T0265787

This Is
Beyond
Budgeting

This Is Beyond Budgeting

A Guide to More Adaptive and Human Organizations

Bjarte Bogsnes

WILEY

Published by John Wiley & Sons, Inc., Hoboken, New Jersey.
Published simultaneously in Canada.

For general information on our other products and services or for technical support, please contact our Customer Care Department within the United States at (800) 762-2974, outside the United States at (317) 572-3993 or fax (317) 572-4002.

Wiley also publishes its books in a variety of electronic formats. Some content that appears in print may not be available in electronic formats. For more information about Wiley products, visit our web site at www.wiley.com.

Library of Congress Cataloging-in-Publication Data

Names: Bogsnes, Bjarte, author.
Title: This is beyond budgeting : a guide to more adaptive and human
   organizations / Bjarte Bogsnes.
Description: Hoboken, New Jersey : John Wiley & Sons, Inc., [2023] |
   Includes index.
Identifiers: LCCN 2022053747 (print) | LCCN 2022053748 (ebook) | ISBN
   9781394171248 (hardback) | ISBN 9781394171255 (adobe pdf) | ISBN
   9781394171637 (epub)
Subjects: LCSH: Management. | Organizational effectiveness. |
   Organizational change. | Organizational behavior. | Organizational
   sociology.
Classification: LCC HD31.2 .B64 2023 (print) | LCC HD31.2 (ebook) | DDC
   658—dcundefined

LC record available at https://lccn.loc.gov/2022053747
LC ebook record available at https://lccn.loc.gov/2022053748

Cover Design: Wiley
Author Photo by Christian Elfstrøm
SKY10039528_120722

For Robin

Contents

Contents

Foreword

Escaping the curse of bureaucracy

Across the globe there is a small but growing band of bold thinkers and doers who are reinventing management from the ground up. Bjarte Bogsnes is one of those rebels. He understands that management—the structures and systems we use to get things done at scale—is one of humankind's most important technologies. He also knows that bureaucracy—the management model that underpins virtually every large organization—is fast becoming a competitive, social, and economic liability. Bureaucracy, with its authoritarian power structures and rule-choked processes is a 19th-century technology and no longer fit for purpose. It was built at a time when most employees were illiterate, when information was expensive to gather and share, and when the pace of change was comparatively glacial. Bureaucracy was built to maximize compliance for the sake of efficiency. But in the 21st century, efficiency is but one advantage among many. Organizations need to be cost-effective, yes, but they must also be adaptable, creative, and purpose-driven. That's why we need a new management model—one that maximizes contribution for the sake of impact.

To build this new management model, we must start by radically reimagining the budgeting process—bureaucracy's central nervous system. It is through the annual budgeting wrangle that priorities get defined, targets get set and resources get allocated. Arguably, no other process has a bigger impact on organizational performance—and at the moment, the performance of many organizations is lackluster at best.

Years ago, with the late C. K. Prahalad, I wrote an article for the *Harvard Business Review* titled "The Core Competence of the Corporation." If I were writing that article today, I would call it "The Core Incompetence of the Corporation." When I look around the world, virtually every large organization is afflicted with the same disabilities: they are timid, inertial, and incremental. Typically, large institutions are content with single percentage point gains in revenue and profit growth. They're reactive and are often years late in intercepting new trends. They invariably overinvest in legacy business while starving new ideas of resources. Budgeting is at the heart of all these failures. As a process, it's a backward-looking, internally focused, and highly politicized. It discourages boldness, perpetuates the past, and rewards mediocrity.

Put simply, we'll never build fundamentally more capable organization unless we raze the traditional budgeting process and build something better in its place. That's why Bjarte's work, and this book, are so important.

The good news is that there are powerful, practical alternatives to budgeting as usual—radical new approaches that can help your organization aim higher, move faster, and take control of its own destiny. The bad news is that changing the way your organization budgets won't be easy. This is true for at least three reasons. First, budgeting is tightly intertwined with other critical processes—like performance management and compensation. You can't change the budgeting process in isolation. Second, budgeting is about power as much as money. Managers index their authority by the size of the budgets they command and compete vigorously to acquire more capital and headcount. In this sense, budgeting is a massive multiplayer game—and those who've learned to play the game well will resist a rule change. Finally, most leaders view the budgeting process as an indispensable tool for exercising control. Budgets are used to enact corporate priorities (by earmarking funds for key initiatives), ensure fiscal discipline (by setting category limits on expenditures), and identify substandard performance (by setting baseline targets). The idea of managing without budgets would strike most managers as something akin to financial suicide.

Overcoming these challenges—complexity, resistance, and fear—is a daunting task. It's why the vast majority of companies are still stuck with Budgeting 1.0. Even those companies that have adopted Beyond Budgeting are mostly "improvers" rather than "transformers"—as Bjarte notes in Chapter 5.

There's a risk, then, that "beyond budgeting" follows the same trajectory as "agile teams." Companies apply the tools without fully embracing the philosophy. They make minor adjustments, fail to follow through, and get disillusioned when the benefits fail to live up to the hype. It's a bit like buying an exercise bike, doing a couple of 15-minute stints, and then being frustrated that you're not yet impressively fit.

Soon the bike is covered in dust, like the yoga mat in the closet and the barbells under the bed.

Given all this, you need to keep one central point in mind as you read this book: the transformative power of Beyond Budgeting is less about tools (as valuable as they are) and more about principles—like purpose, transparency, autonomy, and trust. Beyond Budgeting isn't a set of techniques for improving the way bureaucracy works; it's a set of principles for upending the bureaucratic status quo and reversing the "controlism" that undermines organizational resilience and creativity. An organization that works diligently to operationalize these principles will end up looking almost nothing like its bureaucratic peers. It will be flatter, leaner, simpler, faster, and radically more empowered.

You will find plenty in this book about how to get from here to there. But for now, let me note that you will need to think both big and small—you'll need an approach that is both revolutionary and evolutionary. Back in the 1960s, putting a human being on the moon was an audacious goal, but Neil Armstrong's "giant leap for mankind" was the culmination of many much smaller steps. So it is with reinventing budgeting. You must first commit to a lofty goal—ridding your organization of bureaucracy and the fiction that more elaborate budgets yield more control—and then find a way of moving forward through small, risk-bounded steps.

As you'll learn, there is nothing conceptually difficult about Beyond Budgeting, nor is there any doubt about the payoff, if you take the idea seriously. Fact is, the challenges of replacing the traditional budget with built-for-purpose processes, while considerable, are relatively modest when compared to a major IT overhaul or a typical, top-down "transformation program."

Nevertheless, the challenge of reshaping executive behaviors and reimagining management processes isn't for the faint-hearted. The journey requires curiosity, audacity, and perseverance. Leaders need to be open to the possibility that tomorrow's most successful organizations will be as different from today's stratified, rule-choked leviathans as YouTube is different from broadcast television or PayPal is different from a checkbook. Leaders must be willing to venture beyond the safe precincts of conventional wisdom and experiment with bold new approaches to planning, target-setting, and control. They must believe, in the deepest recesses of their hearts, that human beings need and deserve organizations that are fundamentally more capable than the ones we have right now—and must be willing to put their shoulder to the plough to make this happen. I hope that's you. If it is, you'll find a heaping portion of encouragement, wisdom, and advice in the pages that follow.

Professor Gary Hamel
London Business School

Acknowledgments

Performance is seldom individual. So often, there is someone next to or behind you who also contributed and someone ahead of you who provided inspiration and guidance. That includes writing books.

The writing process has not been a lonely one. A big thank you for great help and feedback goes to my fellows at the Beyond Budgeting Institute: Anders Olesen, Dag Larsson, Steve Morlidge, Rikard Olsson, and Franz Röösli, and to Sebastian Becker at HEC Paris.

Nothing would have happened without my many wonderful colleagues at Borealis and Equinor, and certainly not without these companies' former CEOs, Svein Rennemo and Eldar Sætre.

I also wish to thank my friends in the "Supporting Agile Adoption" group.

And last, but not least. A big thank you to Gary Hamel for writing the foreword and for inspiring so many for so long.

Introduction

My Beyond Budgeting Journey

"I may not have gone where I intended to go, but I think I ended up where I needed to be," Douglas Adams once wrote. This is the story of my life.

I graduated from business studies in the early 1980s, after a short flirt with a military career. My first management job after joining Norwegian Statoil (now Equinor, one of Scandinavia's largest companies) was as head of the corporate budget department. I have led more budgeting rounds than I want to remember in that and in many later finance roles. Looking back, I have done some quite stupid things in my career. But it also means that I know what I am talking about. I have been there and done that. I know most of the tricks in the budget game, including some quite nasty ones.

There was nothing back then indicating that I would become a vocal opponent of this management concept and the philosophy behind it. I have now been one for almost 30 years. I am still embarrassed about an interview I gave to the in-house company magazine, praising the brilliance of budgeting. I hope there are no more copies around!

It all started in the mid-1990s at Borealis, at the time Europe's largest petrochemicals company. The company was partly owned by Statoil and headquartered in Copenhagen. I headed up the corporate finance team. We were all challenged to think of new, different, and better ways of doing our work and of running the company. Our proposal to kick out the budget felt scary. We had not heard of anyone else doing this. We got a "yes," provided we could find an alternative. Beyond Budgeting was not yet born, so we went looking for possible solutions.

After a lot of searching (no Google back then!), many discussions, and some dead ends, we finally cracked it. "Why do we budget?" was the simple question we needed to ask. The answer, which I will return to later, provided us with all we needed. Borealis became one of the inspirations for Jeremy Hope (RIP) and Robin Fraser, the founders of the Beyond Budgeting Roundtable. I later became the chairman of this international network of organizations and individuals interested in Beyond Budgeting.

After heading up finance, I moved to a similar role in human resources before returning to Statoil. I am probably one of very few having worked in both these functions. Those HR years had a big influence on my Beyond Budgeting journey. I will revert to why the two need to work much more closely together.

In my new role as corporate controller for Statoil's international business I could not resist challenging my colleagues on the budget management we were running. In 2004 we went together to the executive committee with a proposal that now had become more ambitious than just kicking out the budget. It was about a new way of leading and managing. The model we proposed, Ambition to Action, has been at the core of the company's performance process ever since. I left my controller role to work full time on Ambition to Action, both on further development and internal training.

The Borealis and Statoil/Equinor cases triggered a lot of external interest. I have been speaking at hundreds of conferences over the years. At Equinor, I also started to run external workshops and do small-scale consulting, with kind permission from my employer. I then made a difficult decision. I left Equinor and started Bogsnes Advisory. I love being able to devote so much more time to Beyond Budgeting, while being a free bird choosing just the work that makes me tick. I seldom have been busier or have had more fun!

Equinor is a great company. I miss my colleagues, and I hope and believe they will take Ambition to Action even further.

I come from a family of teachers. My father, my mother, and my sister all made a difference in so many people's life. My finance education took me in a different direction, but I now feel I am back in the fold. I ended up where I needed to be.

I also married a teacher!

Why This Book?

Some of you might know that I already authored two books. *Implementing Beyond Budgeting* was published in 2008 and later in a significantly revised second edition in 2016. These books are about Beyond Budgeting, great cases, and my own journey and implementation experiences.

So why another book?

The previous books have done well, with readers all over the world. These include executives and senior managers. I know because of nice feedback from many of them. Still, they represent a minority of my readers, for the simple reason that they are terribly busy people. There are so many great books out there. Reading them all is a luxury few can squeeze into hectic schedules. If you are one of them, this is on purpose a short book, something that could be read on a flight, for instance, one of the few occasions left without meetings and phone calls.

My own insights and experiences keep evolving. I have now worked with even more great organizations and have written several articles that this book also draws on. So much has happened since the last book; I just have to share it!

The pressure on executive teams today is immense. They keep being challenged by stakeholders about the need for change and radical transformation. The pressure is not just about becoming greener and more sustainable. It is also about becoming more dynamic and adaptive. There is a jungle of models and thousands of books claiming to have the answer. No wonder many feel overwhelmed and confused.

Many respond by embarking on an agile transformation journey. Most discover that agile wasn't designed as a way to run an organization. Its original purpose was to improve how software was developed and how teams worked, which it did, very successfully. But when scaling agile, its "holes" become visible.

Beyond Budgeting fills these holes because it was intended and designed as an agile way of managing an organization. Many companies on transformation journeys are therefore reaching out to us. I hope this book can help even more executive teams understand that there can be no true agile transformation without Beyond Budgeting.

The same goes for Lean, which was born in manufacturing. Lean has also many similarities with Beyond Budgeting, such as trusting those closest to the situation to make the right decisions. But when scaling to enterprise Lean, holes appear also here. Again, Beyond Budgeting can fill these.

The COVID-19 pandemic was an eye-opener for many about the shortcomings of traditional and budget-based management. Seldom have so many budgets become irrelevant so fast. We have faced turmoil before, but the pandemic was different. Earlier times, for instance, the 2008 financial crisis, challenged only one of the assumptions behind traditional management: that the future is predictable and plannable. So many working from home during the pandemic challenged also the second assumption: that people can't be trusted. But they could! A few anecdotal examples of the opposite carry no credible evidence.

I am writing these words as a horrible war is raging in Ukraine, global supply chains are broken, and inflation is raging. No one expected this to happen, and no one has a clue about what will happen next. Once again, organizations all over the world must rapidly change their plans.

All these developments over many years have created a surge in interest for Beyond Budgeting, also among the major consulting firms. Almost all have reached out for a cooperation in some form or shape because their clients are getting interested.

We come from different places, and we might have different agendas. Still, we need these firms on board. They have channels and muscles we don't have. Some of them have been clear about their intention of offering Beyond Budgeting to their clients in any case.

We are not naive, but we have decided to join forces to help them understand what Beyond Budgeting really is about and to avoid implementations being reduced to rolling forecasting exercises or just a more dynamic resource allocation. We have unfortunately seen a few examples. We would rather help these firms and their clients get it right than stand by and watch them fail. Hopefully, this book can help both in reaching a deeper and better understanding of Beyond Budgeting.

By the way, if you wonder who "we" are, check out the Epilogue.

If you are new to Beyond Budgeting and this book triggers your interest, my previous books have more of everything, including extensive case stories about Borealis, Equinor, and others. There are also other books to learn from. *Beyond Budgeting*, written by Jeremy Hope and Robin Fraser in 2003, is a classic. I also recommend Steve Morlidge's great books on a range of Beyond Budgeting topics. Check also out *The Viable Map Workbook* published by the Beyond Budgeting Institute. More about the Viable Map and the book in Chapter 8.

I am sure you are curious about what you need to do differently when going Beyond Budgeting. Don't worry; you will get it. There is no rocket science. But changing what we do helps little unless we also change how we think. This is the hardest part and should be your most important reason for reading this book.

If you already read any of my books, you may recognize some messages and stories. The purpose of this one is to condense these and make them more accessible for busy people, while also sharing new experiences and insights. I sincerely hope those who need to read it find the time. For those already onboard, but your managers or colleagues aren't, maybe this book could help?

As you may know, or will discover, Beyond Budgeting is about much more than budgets. It is a comprehensive model, addressing both leadership principles and management processes, and the importance of coherence between the two. Believing that Beyond Budgeting is just about budgets is as wrong as believing that agile is just about software. Beyond Budgeting challenges traditional management, which has the budgeting process and the budgeting mindset of prediction and distrust at its core. Hence the name.

Many have challenged us about finding a better name. We are open to it, but only if a new one is significantly better. If you have a proposal, please let us know!

In the meantime, we will stick with Beyond Budgeting. It has become a brand. It creates attention, and even provokes some. If we can use this attention to explain what Beyond Budgeting really is about, then the name might have served its purpose.

This book starts with reflections on a few topics I find intriguing, a warm-up to what follows. What does "control" really mean, for instance?

We take a closer look at the many problems associated with the budgeting process and the budgeting mindset, before we move to Beyond Budgeting as a solution to these and many other traditional management problems, including those associated with targets. Individual bonus amplifies these problems, so I can't help having another go at this flawed management idea. And by the way, do we really need targets? That important question will also be explored.

We then discuss who Beyond Budgeting is for, who is on the journey, and a question we keep getting: Can Beyond Budgeting work in the public sector? Spoiler alert! The answer is "yes."

As discussed, there are many similarities between Beyond Budgeting and agile. The budget is the elephant in the room on agile transformation journeys. This overlooked fact will be addressed. We will also look at similarities, differences, and issues with OKRs (objectives and key results) and with psychological safety. Let me already now make it clear that the full potential of OKRs can never be achieved without doing something with the competition, the budget.

It is impossible to omit the Beyond Budgeting pioneer Handelsbanken, which I also wrote about in my first books. Here comes a new and different take on their amazing and unique management model, including a great story from one of its UK branch offices.

We will finish with reflections and advice on implementation, and two important questions: "What's in it for the bottom line?" and "What's in it for me?"

You may at times find me provocative. I am, with the best conscience because nothing here is grabbed out of thin air. If you are skeptical, the only thing I ask for is to give me a chance. I hope you find the time, not just to start but also to finish reading this book. If you disagree, fair enough.

I still hope this will resonate with you. It is nothing but common sense.

Chapter 1

Initial Reflections

The Innovation Paradox

Everybody loves innovation. Organizations want to be at the leading edge, always ahead. Everybody is encouraged to think outside the box (which can be hard if you are stuck in one. . .). The innovation enthusiasm is, however, very technology oriented on products, services, and customer offerings. *Technology innovation* is a crowded place because everybody is into it.

But the love has its limits. When we move to *management innovation*, exploring new ways of leading and managing, the enthusiasm seems to fade. "Losing control? Are you crazy!" Management innovation is therefore not yet a crowded place because it seems scary.

Few realize what great news this is for brave companies that dare to explore and embrace also this kind of innovation. There is just as much competitive advantage to be gained from management innovation as there is from technology innovation. Handelsbanken and many others are crystal clear about their source of competitive advantage. They find it in the way they lead and manage, not in what they produce, sell, or provide.

The Illusion of Control

While losing control is one of the biggest fears in management, having control is one of the biggest illusions.

When I ask executives, managers, finance people, and others to be more concise about their fear of losing control, many go quiet after having mentioned cost control. They struggle with defining what they are so afraid of losing.

Oxford Dictionary defines *control* as "the power to influence people's behavior or the course of events." In organizational terms this means controlling people and controlling the future. We are back to traditional management beliefs. People can't be trusted, and the future is predictable and plannable. Having next year described with a million details and decimals might feel comfortable but actually provides little control. "More fiction has been written in Excel than in Word," as Daniel Pink put it.

Does hitting the bottom-line budget number mean that we have control if we could have done better? Or staying within the cost budget if we could have spent less or should have spent more?

If we don't have control, whatever it means, it is better to acknowledge it and act accordingly than to fool ourselves by believing we have it and act accordingly. And remember, trust is free; control is not. Do the math. (See Figure 1.1)

People are not stupid. Most control mechanisms can be cheated if people really want to. And, how come so many want to control, while so few want to be controlled?

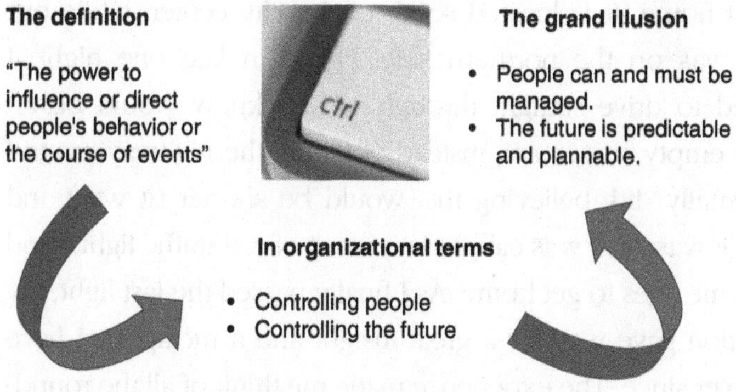

The definition

"The power to influence or direct people's behavior or the course of events"

The grand illusion

- People can and must be managed.
- The future is predictable and plannable.

In organizational terms

- Controlling people
- Controlling the future

Figure 1.1 The illusion of control.

The more volatility and uncertainty there is in our business environment, and the more competent employees are, the more different and better control mechanisms are needed, and the more self-regulating the management model must be. We will revert to this simple but important insight.

A final comment. When Beyond Budgeting challenges "command and control," it is more about control than command. Command isn't necessarily a problem if it is about creating direction and rallying people to a common purpose.

Can We Learn from Traffic Control?

Here is a story and a metaphor that might help you better understand the Beyond Budgeting philosophy.

Borealis, where my Beyond Budgeting journey started, had manufacturing plants all over Europe, so my work involved a lot of traveling. Copenhagen Airport sometimes felt like a second home. It is located south of the city center, while our home was on the northern side. Flying in late one night, I decided to drive straight through what I knew would be an almost empty city center, instead of taking the highway around as I usually did, believing this would be shorter (it was) and faster (it wasn't). I was caught in a wave of red traffic lights, and it took me ages to get home. As I finally passed the last light, my frustration gave way for a great insight and a metaphor I have used ever since. The experience made me think of all the round-abouts being built in my Norwegian hometown of Stavanger.

Managing organizations and managing traffic share a common purpose, namely, good performance. In traffic, this means a safe and good flow, especially where there is crossing traffic. I really dislike waiting for green lights (because there is a much better alternative) and being stuck in traffic jams. It is such a waste of time. I have by the way never understood why it's called the rush hour. There is no rush at all; those cars are standing dead still!

Have you ever wondered why roundabouts are usually much more effective than traffic lights? Please note that I am thinking about programmed lights here, not those with sensors. By the way, roundabouts are also safer and have lower life cycle costs.

The reason is that in a roundabout drivers decide when to drive and when to stop, using fresh, real-time information to make their decisions. In front of a traffic light, a program-mer has made these decisions, based on information that never will be entirely fresh. And where would that person be as you sit there waiting? I never checked, but I don't think there is anyone inside that pole.

It is not enough to have access to fresh information and the authority to act on it. A mindset of "Me first, I don't care about the rest" is seldom a problem in front of a light because it (hopefully) is overruled by red. In the roundabout, however, this would be a serious problem. Here, we are dependent on drivers sharing a common wish of wanting traffic to flow well. We must help each other and interact with each other in a very different way than needed when waiting for the green light. Beyond *fresh information* and the *authority* to act, we need *collaboration*.

But what about the police officer, waiving and whistling in the middle of the crossing? That person would also have access to fresh information and the authority to act on it? Sure, but who needs that middle manager when the roundabout can do the job both better and cheaper?

Trust is obviously a key theme here. In front of the light, we are not trusted to make decisions; in the roundabout, we are. Whom we need to trust also differs. Approaching the light, we must trust the programmer and the hardware. In the roundabout, we must trust the other drivers.

Transparency is another key theme. The only transparency required while waiting for green is the ability to see the color of the light. In the roundabout, we need to see and understand the entire situation.

Finally, driving in a roundabout requires more from us than when responding to a light. It takes more *competence*.

Going back to our organizations, everything we need to leave behind of traditional management thinking and practices are much easier for everybody involved compared to what we need to move toward. Take budgets. Managers know exactly what performance is expected from them, how much they are allowed to spend, and on what. Hit your numbers, and you are fine. Finance believes the job is done when budget variances are explained. Beyond Budgeting requires more from us. We should not go because it is easier; we should go because it makes us perform better and in the right way. It makes us more adaptive and more human. It makes work more fulfilling, and it makes us more attractive as employers.

These traffic control alternatives are based on two very different philosophies, despite having the same purpose. The roundabout is a *self-regulating* way of managing, a good control mechanism, as opposed to the strict, rules-based red/ green bad control. Beyond Budgeting replaces bad controls with good controls. I wouldn't call that losing control.

I am quite sensitive about language in what we are discussing here. There are some corporate phrases I really dislike. One is "performance management." I find it very negative. Aren't we telling people that "If we don't manage your performance, there will be no performance"? I also believe there are illusions of control at play here. Our ability to "manage performance" in today's business and people realities is much lower than many like to think.

I am also no fan of "human resources." And the "corporate controller" desperately needs a new name!

Still, the performance management label makes very much sense when we talk about traffic lights. This is exactly what traffic authorities are doing: they are managing performance, very directly. Roundabouts, however, are about something else. Here it is about *creating conditions* for great performance to take place. It is about *enabling* performance, not managing it.

This is more than playing with words. These are two fundamentally different ways of approaching that big question: how do we achieve the best possible performance in our organizations? The question is not new; it has always been with us. It is the answers that have changed.

Still, so many want to manage, and so few want to be managed. When was the last time you longed for someone to manage your performance?

"Management" has over the years been added to everything, not just performance. Change management, quality management, risk management. The list is long. Because it sounds more managerial, more macho? Nowadays, "agile" is being put in front of everything, with the best of intentions but with the risk of watering out a great idea. More about agile later.

Performance can't be managed. You can sow the seeds and nurture the soil, but you can't make a flower grow by pulling on it. And you don't dig it up once a month to check how the roots are growing.

Key Takeaways

- We love technology innovation but fear management innovation.
- So many struggle with describing the control they are so afraid of losing.
- So many fail to understand the illusions of control.
- The roundabout is much more efficient than traffic lights because it is self-regulating; drivers make decisions based on fresh information. It requires more transparency, more competence, and stronger values.
- Performance can be enabled, but not managed.

Chapter 2

The Problem

The Problems with Budgets and Budgeting

Many will probably think about budgets mainly as cost or project budgets. The finance definition is broader, and it includes annual profit and loss, investment, cash flow and balance sheet budgets, and often related sales and production budgets.

In Beyond Budgeting, the term *budgeting* is not only used in a finance sense, but also as a more generic term for command and control management, with the annual budget process at its core. In this context it describes both a leadership culture and a management system.

It is now time to take a closer look at the many problems this way of thinking and managing creates, which I have so far only been hinting at, beyond the illusion of control problem we just discussed. There is probably no management process people dislike more. Maybe performance appraisals come close. Here are the most common complaints we hear:

- Making and following up on budgets is very time-consuming. I recall a visit to a French company some years ago. Its budgeting process started in March and wasn't finished before next March. Maybe that is why it is called the annual budget! Some years ago, the Hackett Group found that the average billion-dollar company spent as many as 25,000 person-days per billion dollars of revenue only putting together the annual budget. That does not include the time spent following up budgets, and the time consumed has not certainly decreased over the years! Some regard this massive amount of time consumed as the biggest problem. I disagree, but it absolutely does belong on the list.

- Making budget assumptions in an increasingly volatile and uncertain world is becoming more and more challenging. The only thing we know for certain about what lies ahead is that we don't know. "The future ain't what it used to be," the American baseball player Yogi Berra once put it. It never was and it never will be.

- The many unethical behaviors triggered by budgeting are a serious problem. Lowballing, sandbagging, resource hoarding, and frenzied December spending is about games being played, and they are not the kind of behaviors we would like to see among colleagues. We should not criticize people behaving like this, though. They are just responding to the system they are told to operate within. If we want to change behaviors, we need to fix systems, not people. "The role of management is to change the system, not badgering individuals to do better" (Deming).

- Budgeting forces us to make decisions way too early—
what we want to do next year, the cost of it, as well as
what good performance looks like 12 months down
the road. Too many of these decisions are taken too
high up, too far away from those closest to the situation with the best information. This seldom improves
the quality of these decisions; often it is the other
way around.
- Budgets make us rigid and can hinder us in doing
things we should have done but can't because it is not
in the budget. And sometimes it might lead us to do
things we maybe shouldn't have done because there
is money left. "Use it or lose it." A cost budget can be
an effective ceiling on cost but is just as effective
as a floor.
- Detailed, cascaded cost budgets are about managerial
distrust. This kind of command and control micromanagement makes no sense in modern knowledge
organizations.
- The fiscal year is often an artificial construct from a
business perspective in its myopic focus on year-end
and the annual update rhythm, which hinders us in
operating on more business and event driven rhythms,
reflecting the pace and volatility of our business
environments.
- Defining good performance as hitting budget numbers
is narrow, mechanical, and often plain wrong. We need
a richer and broader performance language and a
more holistic performance evaluation.

I have been sharing this list of problems with hundreds of thousands of people all over the world. The response is always the same. So many nodding heads and guilty smiles. Are there, by the way, any of these problems you haven't experienced in your own organization?

Why do most organizations then continue doing what most of them agree isn't very smart, even if that fortunately is changing these days?

I have a few theories. But let me first add a final problem, which surprisingly few recognize and have on their list. It goes back to the important question that cracked it all for us in Borealis and helped us get started in Equinor. It has over the years also helped many other organizations getting started.

"Why do we budget?" This is a question with more than one answer. As we will come back to discuss, the budget has several conflicting purposes. This is a special problem; it also provides solutions for many of the other problems we just discussed.

Back to my theories about why so many continue doing what they admit doesn't make much sense. One reason is the belief that everybody else is doing it, which isn't true anymore. Some managers might also have built their career on mastering the budget game. There is obviously also the fear of losing control.

I believe, however, the main reason is that these problems are regarded simply as irritating itches, and not as what they really are, namely, symptoms of a serious and systemic underlying problem, which also is a paradox.

Budgeting is an old management technology. James O. McKinsey first described the concept in his book *Budgetary*

Control published in 1922. His intentions were the best: to help companies perform better. This was management innovation that worked well back then, and maybe even 50 years ago. Today, however, things have changed: both our business environments and people's competence and capability. Today, this way of thinking and this way of managing is doing exactly the opposite. It has become more of a barrier than a support for unleashing performance.

A 2016 *Management Lab* article by Gary Hamel and Michele Zanini ("The $3 Trillion Prize for Busting Bureaucracy [and How to Claim It]") confirms many of the problems we have discussed:

- Only 17% of the managers polled by the *Wall Street Journal* believed their budget process is effective.
- 60% of companies in the same survey reported that their annual budget targets became obsolete by the second quarter.
- 46% of senior finance professionals in an ACCA/KPMG study believed their budget is a politically agreed number generated from the top and not linked to business reality.
- Only 32% of companies in a McKinsey study rate their capital allocation process as very or extremely effective.
- 95% of managers in a Corporate Executive Board survey are dissatisfied with their performance management process.

If you were in doubt about the seriousness of the problems we are facing, I hope these numbers make you reconsider and maybe accept that we are not looking at a trivial problem. It won't be solved until we change how we think and not only what we do.

The Citizen-Employee Paradox

Let us close this chapter with a reflection on something that is both a paradox and a problem. It is fascinating to observe how much schizophrenia there is in our lives, and how little we seem to reflect on it.

As citizens in a free society, we take for granted that we should elect our leaders, that big decisions require referendums, and that there should be full transparency about public spending. It is blindingly obvious that nobody else should or could make big decisions in our lives about education, marriage, having children, or buying a home. It would feel strange if there only would be one source and one time slot a year for funding that last decision. We all try to spend our money as wisely as possible. We have few problems buying stuff online from people we have never met. And don't detailed five-year plans sound very much like what the Soviet Union failed so miserably with?

What happens then when we go to work in the morning? Suddenly, our belief system turns 180 degrees because the employee hat now is on. Now we seem completely fine with the very opposite. Managers must be appointed from above. Big decisions can only be made by executives. Travel and stationery purchases must be pre-approved. No one should know what others spend. There can be no other funding source than the budget, once a year only, and of course, we need to spend all of it. We can't buy from someone without credit checks and purchase orders. And how would we know where to go and what to do unless there is a five-year business plan?

Some of you might argue that these two sides of our lives are very different. Organizations and businesses are more complex and involve handling other people's money, right? Well, private decisions can also be complex and difficult. And when it comes to money, organizations have a lot to learn from the cost consciousness and frugality people apply in their private spending, as we will discuss later.

The way to address this paradox, of course, should be about changing employee life more toward resembling that of free citizens. Unfortunately, in an increasing number of autocratic countries, the opposite is happening. These have narrowed the gap by moving in the opposite direction. Here, leaders are no longer elected. There are no fair referendums and no spending transparency whatsoever. Trust is limited to family and no one else. Even whom to love and whom to marry is not always a private decision. Such a sad and wrong way of addressing paradoxes and closing gaps.

A final reflection. When it comes to the military, it all comes together, at least for the labels we use. Companies organize themselves in divisions, leaders are called officers, battlegrounds are chosen, and the front line is where the casualties are.

Key Takeaways

- The complaints about budgeting are very much the same across businesses, geographies, and cultures. Still, most organizations continue doing what most of them admit isn't very smart.
- Few acknowledge the serious and systemic problem behind. What was once developed to help organizations perform better is today doing the very opposite.
- The gap between what we expect as free citizens and what we accept as employees is part of the problem.

Chapter 3

Beyond Budgeting

The Model and the Principles

As already discussed, traditional management is built on the assumptions that the future is predictable and plannable, and that people can't be trusted. Beyond Budgeting challenges both. Few would today agree on the first assumption because finance crises, pandemics, and wars and much else have shattered most remaining illusions of predictability.

When it comes to people, the jury still seems to be out. Although work has changed and become more complex and less "manageable," many seem to hang on to beliefs and practices belonging to a different time.

The management thinkers Peter Drucker and Russel L. Ackoff had some wonderful reflections on these assumptions.

> "Most of what we call management is about making it difficult for people to do their job". (Drucker)
>
> "Most corporate planning is like a ritual rain dance. It has no effect on the weather, but those who engage in it think it does. Much of the advice and instruction is directed at improving the dancing, not the weather" (Ackoff). See Figure 3.1.

"Most corporate planning is like a ritual rain dance. It has no effect on the weather, but those who engage in it think it does. Much of the advice and instruction is directed at improving the dancing, not the weather."

Figure 3.1 The corporate rain dance.

The Beyond Budgeting model and the first version of its 12 principles was developed by Jeremy Hope and Robin Fraser in the late 1990s, based on what they observed in several companies. These had all challenged budgeting and traditional management. What the two found in these companies was not entirely identical, neither the problems they were trying to solve nor what they did instead. It was, however, similar enough to inspire the Beyond Budgeting model and its principles.

Discovering Handelsbanken was key, realizing that it was about much more than budgets. Hope and Fraser also discovered Borealis (actually, I discovered them). Their visits to Copenhagen became the start of my involvement with the

Beyond Budgeting movement and the Beyond Budgeting Roundtable, which was established a few years later.

Beyond Budgeting was not born in the consulting business or in academia. It came from practitioners being frustrated with, and rebelling against, the serious shortcomings of traditional management, with the budgeting process and mindset at its core.

I believe this is one of the reasons why the concept resonates so well with managers and employees all over the world. They recognize the tangible problem description and they get the new way, although it does take time for some.

Beyond Budgeting is not academic theory alone or a commercial and consultant-driven certification machine. The Core Team (See Epilogue) are people passionate about the model, "pragmatic radicals" as one of them labels himself.

The 12 principles have evolved over the years, but the philosophy hasn't changed. Today, they are expressed as described in Figure 3.2.

Observant readers might have noticed a few recent, minor revisions. The new subtitle *"Performance. The Right Way."* has an important message. Beyond Budgeting changes how we define and deliver performance.

The adjustments involve a few changes in the order of the principles, and the "Performance evaluation" text has been adjusted to better reflect that the principle addresses both performance measurement and final performance evaluation. The "Rhythm" principle has been renamed "Coordination."

There might be nothing unique about the leadership principles in Beyond Budgeting. Much research, and many

Beyond Budgeting.
Performance. The right way.

Leadership principles	Management processes
1. **Purpose** - Engage and inspire people around bold and noble causes; *not around short-term financial targets*	7. **Targets** - Set directional, ambitious and relative goals; *avoid fixed and cascaded targets*
2. **Values** - Govern through shared values and sound judgement; *not through detailed rules and regulations*	8. **Forecasts** - Make forecasting a lean and unbiased process; *not a rigid and political exercise*
3. **Transparency** - Make information open for self-regulation, innovation, learning and control; *don't restrict it*	9. **Resource allocation** - Foster a cost conscious mind-set. Plan and make resources available as needed; *not through detailed annual budget allocations*
4. **Autonomy** - Trust people with freedom to act; *don't punish everyone if someone should abuse it*	10. **Performance evaluation** - Evaluate performance holistically to guide interventions; *not based on measurement only and not for rewards only*
5. **Organisation** - Cultivate a strong sense of belonging and organise around accountable teams; *avoid hierarchical control and bureaucracy*	11. **Rewards** - Reward shared success against competition; *not against fixed performance contracts*
6. **Customers** - Connect everyone's work with customer needs; *avoid conflicts of interest*	12. **Coordination** - Organise management processes dynamically around business rhythms and events; *not around the calendar year only*

Figure 3.2 The Beyond Budgeting principles.
Source: Beyond Budgeting Institute.

This Is Beyond Budgeting

other communities, have similar views and recommendations. What is often missing, however, are reflections on what kind of *management processes* are required to activate good leadership intentions.

The "Organization" principle deserves, however, a comment. Beyond Budgeting is quite agnostic when it comes to organizational structure. The model can in principle work in any structure, even where the organization chart looks hierarchical, multilayered, and siloed. Equinor might fall in this category, but its organization chart says nothing about the low power distance, the transparency, and all the collaboration across the company. I believe formal structures often are given too much emphasis. Many seem to believe that the answer lies in copying the "Spotify model" of squads, tribes, and chapters.

A final reflection on structure. The matrix organization is sometimes criticized for being ineffective. I don't fully appreciate the problem. Many of us actually grew up in one, being raised by two parents.

Back to leadership. Douglas McGregor's book *The Human Side of Enterprise* and his Theory X and Theory Y are just as relevant today as when it was published back in 1960. As you might be familiar with, McGregor described two contrasting models on employee motivation. Theory X has an authoritarian approach, with a belief that people will not perform unless they are instructed, tightly managed, and rewarded or punished. Theory Y has a more human and participative approach; most people want to do a good job, they want to be listened to, they want to be involved and be treated as adults.

Today, most of us hopefully would subscribe to Theory Y more than Theory X. But it doesn't help having Theory Y leadership visions if there are Theory X management processes. The result is poisonous gaps between what is preached and what is practiced, as sadly seen in so many organizations.

Likewise, there are other management process models out there, but with a similar lack of reflections about what kind of leadership is needed to underpin and inspire the design of these processes.

Beyond Budgeting focuses on both and on the need for a horizontal coherence between the two, between what is said and what is done. It doesn't help with warm statements about "What fantastic employees we have! We would be nothing without you, and we trust you so much!" if there are detailed travel budgets. Another classic example: equally warm words about teamwork, collaboration, and everybody being in the same boat, but when it comes to rewards, it is all about individual bonus.

This is pure hypocrisy. Even the best leadership intentions become hollow when management processes have the very opposite message. What we do always speaks louder than what we say.

The model also emphasizes the need for a vertical coherence, especially between the management processes target setting, forecasting, resource allocation, performance evaluation, and rewards. It must all hang together, speak the same language, and be built on the same philosophy. This is one of several reasons why finance and human resources should work closely together in designing and supporting the new performance process. More about this later.

Finally, Beyond Budgeting addresses the need for coherence with the organization's external environment. A management model must enable the organization to adapt at least as fast as its environment changes. See Figure 3.3.

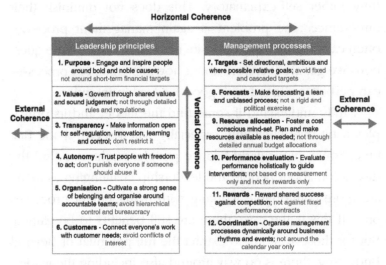

Figure 3.3 Beyond Budgeting coherence.

Ross Ashby, a British cybernetic theorist working to understand self-regulating biological systems in the 1950s defined what has become known as Ashby's law. The variety or complexity of the environment must not exceed the systems' (the management model's) capacity to deal with it. If it does, the system dies.

Or, as it also has been said, "In order to deal properly with the diversity of problems the world throws at you, you need to have a repertoire of responses that are at least as nuanced as the problems you face" (John Naughton).

Why Do We Budget?

Let us now take a closer look at the origins of some of the Beyond Budgeting principles. The six on leadership are hopefully rather self-explanatory. This does not diminish their importance. The problem is again management processes often carrying the very opposite messages. Many of the questions we get are therefore about how management processes can be better aligned with good leadership intentions.

I fully understand if some find the model and its principles a bit overwhelming, especially when seen for the first time. Some, particularly finance people, might also find the discussion about people and leadership challenging as many are more comfortable working with management processes only. If this is the case, there are still benefits to be gained. But for those wanting to extract the full potential of Beyond Budgeting, there is no way around also including the leadership side. That is why we so strongly encourage finance to join forces with their human resources colleagues on these important issues. More about this when we later discuss Beyond Budgeting for both "improvers" and "transformers."

Although it is possible to work on the management process side only, the opposite is hard, if not impossible. Addressing the leadership side only, with little or no implications for management processes, is at the best wishful thinking, at the worst pure hypocrisy.

For those feeling overwhelmed, there is, however, a place to start that is not big and not scary. It is about management processes. It is pure logic, and it provides a platform for later and bigger Beyond Budgeting discussions. We are back to the question raised several times already: "Why do we budget?"

Almost everybody answering this question comes up with same three main reasons. The budget is used for setting *targets*—financial, sales, or production. But it shall also provide a *forecast* of what we believe lies ahead in terms of profit, cash flow, and financial capacity. Finally, the budget has a *resource allocation* purpose, handing out bags of money for expenditures and investments. Targets are again used for *performance measurement, evaluation, and rewards*. Budgets are also about *coordination*, the rhythm we run our management processes on.

If you miss *planning* here, I will explain why in the "Forecasting" section in Chapter 4. Remember that a plan is a combination of words and numbers, of actions and forecasts. What we discuss here is mainly about the budget numbers.

Handling target setting, forecasting, and resource allocation in one process and one set of numbers might seem very efficient. But herein lies the problem because these are conflicting purposes.

Imagine the start of a budget process, when finance wants to understand next year's profit and cash flow. Starting with revenues, managers are asked for their best numbers. Everybody knows that what is sent upstairs tends to come back as targets, often with a bonus attached. We all know what this insight can do to submitted numbers.

Moving to expenditures and investments, everybody knows this is the only chance of securing resources for next year, and some might also remember last year's 20% cut. Again, we should not be surprised if this insight and this memory also influences what is sent upstairs.

Although we all recognize the game, most smile and shrug it off as "that's just the way it is." But this is not funny; it is actually a serious problem, and not just because this game destroys the quality of numbers, but even more because it stimulates behaviors that are at least borderline unethical. Lowballing, sandbagging, and resource hoarding are not the behaviors we want to experience with colleagues. I am still not blaming anyone for behaving like this. It is the consequence of a chosen system. Again, we must fix the system, not people.

Fortunately, there is a simple, effective, and tested solution to this problem. The three purposes should be *separated* and then solved in three different processes because they are about different things. A target is an *aspiration*, what we want to happen. A forecast is an *expectation*, what we think will happen, whether we like what we see or not. And resource allocation is about *optimization* of scarce resources.

By separating, we allow for different numbers depending on the purpose. A target can now be more ambitious than a forecast, as it typically should be. But even more important, the separation opens for significant improvement opportunities in each process. We can now make our targets more ambitious, inspiring, and robust. We can take the politics out of forecasting, and we can make our resource allocation much more effective. We can also improve how we measure, evaluate, and reward performance. And finally, we can let each process run on a rhythm much better suited to each purpose and to the kind of business we are in.

This does not involve three times more work, on the contrary. The main benefit still lies in improved quality and to a lesser extent in reduced workload. We will spend our time very differently, on much more fulfilling and value-adding work.

I have helped numerous organizations get started on a Beyond Budgeting journey. Most of them started with purpose separation as described in Figure 3.4. This often becomes a catalyst for later and more fundamental discussions. Target setting: What really motivates people? Forecasting: What really causes the bias and the politics? Resource allocation: Do we need detailed cost budgets if we say that we trust people? The separation is a safe and organic backdoor into broader Beyond Budgeting discussions.

Some tell me it is impossible to operate without a budget. My response is that this separation lets us do everything the budget tried to do for us, but now in much better ways: better targets, better forecasts, and a more effective resource allocation. It also improves how we measure, evaluate, reward, and coordinate. How impossible and how scary is that?

Many point to banks and regulators requiring budgets and investors needing performance guiding. The first ask for budgets because there used to be nothing else to ask for.

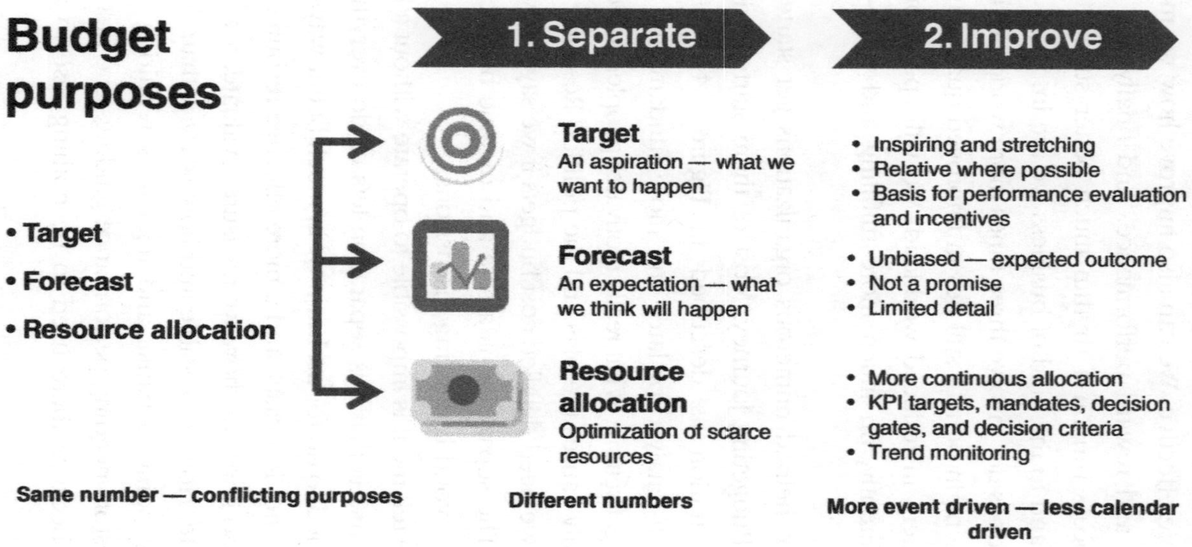

Budget purposes

- Target
- Forecast
- Resource allocation

1. Separate

Target
An aspiration — what we want to happen

Forecast
An expectation — what we think will happen

Resource allocation
Optimization of scarce resources

Same number — conflicting purposes

Different numbers

2. Improve

- Inspiring and stretching
- Relative where possible
- Basis for performance evaluation and incentives

- Unbiased — expected outcome
- Not a promise
- Limited detail

- More continuous allocation
- KPI targets, mandates, decision gates, and decision criteria
- Trend monitoring

More event driven — less calendar driven

Figure 3.4 Budget purpose separation.

This Is Beyond Budgeting

Now we can provide them with an unbiased, reliable forecast and maybe also our targets. They will be more than happy. As for external market guiding, having a quality forecast as the basis for guiding is much more comfortable than having to rely on polluted budget numbers for which we seldom know which purpose dominates: target, forecast, or resource allocation?

The board is also seen as someone requiring budgets. I have, however, yet to meet a board that didn't appreciate the many benefits we just discussed. The Equinor board hasn't requested a budget since it was introduced to Ambition to Action back in 2005. This even goes for new board members. They quickly get it and quickly appreciate it.

These external bodies are often used as excuses and barriers for not going Beyond Budgeting. They are not. There are challenges and barriers, but these are all internal, and they are all in our heads. Again, we need to change how we think.

Changing what we do can sometimes help us think differently. We need new mental models to address the two main questions that Beyond Budgeting ultimately boils down to: *How do we define performance* and *how can we best enable the organization to deliver that performance?*

Let us now explore how each of the budget purposes and related processes can be improved to achieve this.

Key Takeaways

- Beyond Budgeting was born among passionate practitioners, not in consulting firms or in academia, although both are now showing a strong interest.
- The future is not predictable and plannable, and most people can be trusted. This requires a change not just in what we do but even more in how we think.
- Coherence is key, between what is said and what is done, between finance and human resources territory, and between the business environment's complexity and the management model's adaptability.
- Beyond the coherence focus, the uniqueness of Beyond Budgeting lies in cracking the budget problems. This does not diminish the importance of the leadership side, which must inspire and guide design of the new management processes.
- Why do we budget? The three purposes of target setting, forecasting, and resource allocation can't be solved in one process and one set of numbers because aspirations, expectations, and resource optimization are different purposes.
- By separating the three, each can be improved in ways impossible when bundled in one process and one set of numbers. Each one can now also be run on a rhythm better reflecting each purpose and also the kind of organization we are.

Chapter 4

Separate and Improve

Here is advice on designing these new ways of working, after separating the budget purposes and preparing to solve each one in new and more tailored processes. You might find many of these quite different, some even radical. Still, this is not theory and wishful thinking. These are practices that all have been tested and applied in different Beyond Budgeting organizations over many years, with very good results. Chapter 9 provides tangible evidence.

Before we move on, let me clarify why the budget purpose separation we just discussed addressed only the three processes of target setting, forecasting, and resource allocation, whereas there are six management process principles. Performance evaluation and rewards are of a somewhat different nature and will now be based on targets instead of budgets. Coordination, the rhythm we run these on, applies to the other five principles.

Again, don't read any of this as instructions, as a cookbook with a Beyond Budgeting recipe. Take this as inspiration. Pick what works best for your organization, although within the implementation recommendations provided in Chapter 8.

Target Setting

I have yet to meet a football/soccer team stating that the ambition for the next season is to score 45 goals and reach 39 points. These are similar to budget targets, and these teams don't think like that. It is all about performing well against, and hopefully better than, the other teams.

This relative way of thinking can also be applied in organizations, replacing absolute budget targets. These can be external targets (us versus peers or competition) or internal (comparing units).

Such comparisons trigger something quite absent in absolute target negotiations, where the focus is on negotiating the lowest performance targets and the highest cost or investment budgets.

I have never come across a team or an organization that says it is completely happy being a fourth-quartile performer. Everybody wants to improve and climb. Ask a group of business unit heads if they all can accept a target of being better than average. They will all sign up, without protest, even if only half of them will make it. Compare this to the intense low-balling and the under-promise and over-deliver mentality seen in budget negotiations.

Since 2005, Equinor has operated with external relative targets on return on capital employed (ROCE) and shareholder return. These metrics might have their issues, but the point here is that the targets are relative, not absolute. It is about aiming for always performing above average on both, among a group of 11 competitors. It matters little if energy prices are high or low because these prices apply to all of them. Relative targets are therefore much more robust and self-regulating than absolute targets. Such targets can also be "evergreen." There is no need for annual resetting. They simply stand until changed. Equinor has had the same target levels, more or less, since 2005. Performance on the two drives the common bonus system for all employees, a concept borrowed with pride from Handelsbanken.

A relative target might be seen as less precise than a 12.7 % target, but it is much more robust and relevant. It doesn't help to hit 12.7% if most competitors are delivering better numbers. Likewise, not achieving it is not necessarily bad performance if competition is doing even worse.

Thinking in relative terms triggers another important discussion. Do we need targets at all? Nobody likes to be laggards, and everybody strives to perform as well as possible. Isn't this what we want? Why do we then need targets? I promise to revert to this important discussion.

Although relative targets are effective in driving performance, the *learning* aspect is just as, or even more, important. Internal benchmarking, even without targets, encourage low-performing units to ask for inspiration and help from better performing units. For this to happen we need help from the reward system. A common bonus system driven by company performance against competition stimulates internal collaboration. The more we help each other, the better the organization performs and the higher bonus for everybody.

Individual bonus does the very opposite. Why help someone who one day may threaten your position and reduce your bonus?

A common bonus scheme will probably not do this job alone. It is necessary, but not sufficient. Other parts of the management model must also encourage and support collaboration.

For learning to take place there is obviously a need for being transparent about relative performance. Transparency is, however, a powerful mechanism that must be applied with wisdom. If it becomes naming and shaming, it doesn't work. Again a reason for positioning benchmarking mainly as a way to learn from each other. The gentle performance pressure will still be there. One alternative is to publicize only those performing above average, while informing those below about their position. These teams will then know whom to contact to improve.

We will return to the bonus topic late. Before we continue with how to set better targets, a final reflection on cost targets.

Cost or investment level targets expressed as absolute numbers are not really targets because hitting them is not about performance. The only competence required is the ability to spell or pronounce *no*. Such targets are only *constraints*. Performance is about how well we *optimize* within a constraint, what we achieve with the money, the input/output relation.

In Borealis, we adopted another version of relative targets. The petrochemicals business is volatile and cyclical.

Market margins between raw materials and finished products vary massively and constantly. Financial performance has nothing to do with riding up and down on these cycles. It is about improving performance independent of external margin levels.

We therefore introduced an internal relative ROCE KPI. For each business unit we calculated the historical relation between market margins and ROCE, which gave us an ROCE baseline for any margin. Performance was then defined as *lifting* the ROCE baseline independent of market developments. Targets were set as, for instance, "Improve ROCE by 0.3% points." We then gave business units full autonomy on how best to do this, by optimizing on all levers driving their ROCE: production volumes, pricing and rebates, costs, investments, and working capital. Major investments still required separate approvals.

But what if it isn't possible to establish relative targets? What if no or just a few comparable competitors exist, or we can't get data, or if internal units are hard to compare, or the Borealis model isn't relevant? Don't worry, going Beyond Budgeting does not depend on the ability to establish relative targets. It just makes it a bit easier.

If no kind of relative target is available, we *can* use absolute targets. We should, if possible, avoid detailed and decimal-loaded numbers. Think instead "toward," "in the range of," and similar metrics. The more absolute targets are, the more important it is to have a holistic performance evaluation, where new information is considered, such as changes in assumptions and headwind/tailwind. More about this later.

A final reflection on the rhythm of target setting. The general Beyond Budgeting advice is to "Organize dynamically around business rhythms and events, not around the calendar year only." For targets, this has implications for time horizons and updating frequencies, which, by the way, don't have to be the same.

Targets should have natural time horizons: shorter if urgent, longer if what we aim for is more complex and time-consuming. There is nothing wrong with end-of-year deadlines, but these should be the exception more than the rule. This also creates a more dynamic updating frequency. New targets are simply set when old ones have been delivered on or when we need to adjust them. There is also the option of evergreen targets, as discussed.

The more absolute targets are, the less robust they are against changes in assumptions. We therefore need mechanisms for target adjustment. This can be addressed in two ways: by changing targets along the way or by sticking to them but taking new information into account when performance is evaluated. The two can also be combined. I recommend always having the latter mechanism in place because there will almost always be new information that needs to be considered. This also reduces the need for continuously having to adjust targets up or down, which obviously should be avoided. Target adjustments should be limited to major and significant events, when there is a strong need for signaling major changes in direction or ambition levels.

If we want to run an annual formal performance evaluation, this is still possible even if targets have other deadlines.

Some targets will already have been delivered on, some might have a year-end deadline coinciding with the evaluation, while some are works-in-progress and we simply review the current status.

A final reflection on a practice that we fortunately are seeing less of but still is highly problematic. A number of listed companies, especially in the United States, provides quarterly guiding. Each quarter, they provide information to the market about what they expect the quarterly results to be. The label *guiding* is misleading. Although it might sound like a forecast, it is more of a commitment or a target, something the company better not miss.

The arguments for doing this is that it improves companies' valuation, helps reduce share price volatility, keeps management teams accountable for performance, and that investors demand it.

FCLTGlobal, a not-for-profit organization that encourages a longer-term focus in business, debunks them all as pure myths. Quarterly guiding does not improve valuation or reduce volatility. Management teams are held accountable for the wrong metrics, and very few investors demand it.

Quarterly guiding creates a short-term focus and leads to decisions that might benefit the quarterly results but hurts long-term value creation. According to a 2016 McKinsey/ FCLTGlobal study, 60% of executives would delay projects and 40% would give discounts to customer to meet the quarterly guiding.

Although the organization still recommends longer-term guiding on KPIs that drives value over time, several listed companies have skipped the practice altogether. It should be no surprise that Handelbanken is one of them. More about this later.

No Targets?

We have discussed how budget purpose separation enables us to improve targets and target setting. Some companies go further. They skip targets. Handelsbanken is one, but not the only example. I am convinced that more will follow.

Although Beyond Budgeting might seem focused on improving targets, the thinking behind no targets is well in line with the philosophy. Getting rid of targets is also a way of improving them.

The world of management is full of myths and rituals. Many seem to have been with us forever and are often explained and justified with "we have always done it like this" or "everybody else is doing it." It feels like targets have always been there, just like budgets. This is not true. If we go back 20 or 30 years, the situation was quite different. Organizations had many fewer targets. They had budgets, which of course, often represented targets. These were, however, mainly financial numbers.

The birth of the balanced scorecard in the 1990s and the recent rejuvenation of OKRs (more about this later) led to a massive increase in non-financial KPIs, leading to a much greater prevalence of measurement and subsequent target setting.

This new way of managing has spread widely, and "new public management" has now led to a highly problematic increase in target setting and reporting also in the public sector. We will discuss the damage caused later.

Along the way, we seem to have forgotten something important: *A target is not the target.* Performance is not about hitting a given number. What we want is *the best possible performance, given the circumstances*. Setting targets is one way of achieving this, but not the only way, and often it is not the best way.

Rituals are not necessarily a problem. Myths are different because they are often not true. There are three strong myths about targets, all seemingly undisputable justifications for this popular management practice:

- "Without targets, employees will not know what to do."
- "Without targets, employees will not be motivated to perform."
- "Without targets, management will not be able to evaluate performance."

These myths are not only disputable but also they are simply not true. I will explain why, but let me first clarify. The targets I challenge here are numerical targets, for example, in the "29.2" category. Very specific and often annual. In addition, they are absolute, not relative. They are also set from above to control and reward (or punish). I have fewer problems with targets people set for themselves to learn and improve, although these can also be problematic if taken too literally.

Separate and Improve

"Without targets, employees will not know what to do." Not true. Words can often provide direction and set expectations more clearly and intelligently than any single number can do.

"Without targets, employees will not be motivated to perform." Not true. Many, including myself, are much more fired up by dreams and visions of where we want to go, igniting our hearts and minds in a very different way than what clinical and decimal-loaded numbers ever will.

"Without targets, managers will not be able to evaluate performance." Not true. This might be the hardest myth to bust, so let us dive a bit deeper here.

A target tries to describe what good performance looks like at some point down the road, for instance, at year-end in the case of an annual target. When there is a lot of uncertainty, this is difficult. Where is the market going? What will competitors do? What about energy prices and exchange rates? We must make assumptions about all these uncertainties. This forces us to be subjective, even if we want to be objective. Yet, when we finally settle on a number, the subjectivity magically disappears. We have now defined what good performance looks like. It has all become more orderly, and we can focus on measuring whether we are hitting that number or not.

What we have just been through, though, is a *premature* performance evaluation, and again a difficult one, due to all the uncertainty that forced us to make all those guesses. Would it not be easier and make more sense to do this job *afterwards* instead, when all the uncertainty is gone? We then know what happened with markets and competitors. We know how energy prices and exchange rates moved, and so much more. Why should we let guesses made more than 12 months ago be the blind judge when we instead can examine fresh facts on the table? There is a huge difference in uncertainty, as illustrated in Figure 4.1.

To put it simply: We know what good performance looks like when we see it. We seldom need the crutches of pre-set targets.

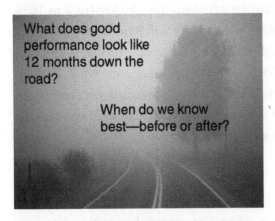

Figure 4.1 Target setting uncertainty.

Many will still argue that targets work. Yes, they do, and that is part of the problem!

Managers hitting their targets is no guarantee that this was the best they could have done. Some might have had a strong tailwind; others, a strong headwind. We only know this in hindsight! Even without a head- or tailwind or changes in assumptions, hitting a target does still not necessarily mean that this was the best performance possible because it assumes that the "right" target was set. We will discuss this further in the "Performance Measurement and Evaluation" section.

Target setting and target delivery might also take place in unwanted ways. As discussed, there is often lowballing and gaming during target negotiations, and equally unethical behaviors when blindly trying to hit them or not exceed them if reached already in November. "The problem is not that we aim too high and miss, but that we aim too low and hit" (Aristotle).

Charles Goodhart reflected on this already back in 1975: "Any observed statistical regularity will tend to collapse once pressure is placed on it for control purposes." Marilyn Strathern later sharpened his message, in what became known as Goodhart's law: *"When a measure becomes a target, it ceases to be a good measure."* It happens because the purpose shifts—from learning to control.

Forecasting

While a budget has several purposes, forecasting has only one: to support decision-making. If you don't know which decisions a forecast shall help you make, you should consider not making one at all.

Beyond Budgeting has several recommendations on forecasting. Before we dive into these, just a clarification on a word you haven't heard me use very much, namely, *planning*. Not because planning isn't important. Of course it is, and going Beyond Budgeting does not mean that we shouldn't plan. We should and must, but in a different and better way.

The budget purpose separation we discussed is about the budget numbers. A plan has two components: words and numbers. The words are about the *actions* we plan to take. The numbers involved are about the expected consequences of these actions. These numbers are *forecasts*. Often, these forecasts will make us revise our actions because we don't like what we see. Many of the following forecast recommendations are just as relevant for the action part.

Let us start with one of the most important ones, and for some, also among the most difficult ones.

Those on the receiving end of forecasts will need to change their behaviors. When faced with a "good forecast with bad news" the response must be "What do you intend to do about it?" and not the budget response of "Come back with better numbers!". Good forecasts can bring bad news. We must not confuse the two.

It is also about rooting out gaming and politics. This will happen only if we remove the reasons for it. By solving target setting and resource allocation in other processes, the forecast is no longer a bid in a target negotiation or an application for resources. It is just a forecast, with no need for gaming it.

This is about removing *bias* from forecasting. Bias is systematic over- or under-forecasting, consciously or unconsciously. It is caused by human behaviors or by poor forecasting models. Bias is different from *variation*, which is unsystematic and often unavoidable. Bias is measured by comparing forecasts to actual outcomes, netting off positive and negative errors. Variation is measured without netting off. For statistical reasons a minimum of four periods are needed.

Measuring forecasting quality only makes sense in the short term. The further out we forecast, the more likely that we use forecasting information to make decisions that intend to change the actual outcome. We can hardly call this bad forecasting. Here, we want to be wrong!

Imagine we are out sailing, and our radar tells us that we are on course to hit a rock. We will use this information to change course. When we hopefully pass the rock safely, we wouldn't blame the radar for providing a bad forecast. Measuring forecasting quality here doesn't make sense because we can influence the outcome.

But assume that we are forecasting tomorrows weather. Tomorrow, we can check our weather forecasting skills. Now, measuring makes sense because we can't influence the outcome.

Beyond Budgeting also has recommendations on forecasting frequency and horizons. Traditional forecasting has an accordion rhythm to it. When budgets are made in the autumn, there is a wish to understand all of next year, 12 months ahead. When the first quarter forecast is made, a nine-month horizon is now sufficient; we can still see till year-end. Later, a six-month and three-month horizon is fine (we can still see till year-end) before we suddenly get interested in 12 months again because it is budget time. It doesn't make much sense!

This is easily solved by introducing rolling forecasts, which typically mean a five-quarter rolling horizon, although some operate with four and some with six quarters. The updating frequency must reflect the type of business we are in, but both monthly and quarterly cycles are quite common. Operational forecasting is typically done even more frequently.

Another question is which *period granularity* to choose, which is different from updating frequency. Many go for quarterly periods, or "buckets," but this depends on what kind of business you are in. In a fast-moving business with short lead times, monthly buckets or even more frequently often make sense. Remember that we need a minimum of four periods to measure forecasting bias. With quarterly periods, we must wait a full year before any bias in the period can be measured.

At Equinor, we implemented what we called *dynamic forecasting*. There is no predefined frequency or time horizon, due to the many different business rhythms across the company. Business units update their forecast when something happens that they themselves believe justifies a forecast update.

These updates should usually not be done just for top management; they should be done to help units manage their own business. Updates are done in a global enterprise system solution. Corporate finance can at any time tap in to retrieve fresh information on the latest forecast status, for instance, on financial capacity ahead of a major investment decision.

There is also no common forecasting time horizon. In the oil trading business, anything beyond three weeks is quite foggy. Why should it be told to forecast a decade ahead, even if this might make sense for a production asset with a 40-year life cycle?

If someone needs a longer forecast than what they get by consolidating numbers from below, they should fill the gap themselves, using their own business understanding instead of requiring data from below with an accounting mindset of "everything must add up from the lowest level."

Beyond Budgeting does not have a strong view on whether a rolling or a dynamic approach is the best solution. Both are within our general recommendation of being more business and event driven and less calendar driven.

Forecasting granularity is also important. When we describe the past through accounting, then details and decimals not only make sense but they also are often required. There is, however, a big difference between describing the past and describing the future. The past carries no uncertainty, whereas the future does. The further ahead we look, the more uncertainty there is. Here, we need to leave the accounting mindset of details, consolidation, and reconciliation behind. We need to not just accept but embrace uncertainty. Ambiguity is not uncomfortable; it is a fact. We need to forget precision and think more in terms of scenarios and ranges.

Sometimes we must even accept that we don't have a clue about what lies ahead. We then need to focus on creating options and agility so that we can move fast when the fog clears.

Dee Hock (RIP), the founder and former CEO of VISA, put it like this: "Certainty is not a property of the universe. It is one of those constructs of the human mind which simply does not exist." And here is Voltaire: "Uncertainty is an uncomfortable position. But certainty is an absurd one."

A final reflection. Sometimes forecasting seems to be about compensating for a lack of agility. Although supertankers need huge radars to reveal what lies ahead, speedboats don't, because they can turn the moment new information emerges. Maybe we should put more efforts into becoming more adaptive and less into becoming better at forecasting?

Some companies, including Handelsbanken, hardly make forecasts. You will hear why later.

Resource Allocation

How can cost be managed without a budget? This is a question we get all the time. I understand why.

Let me start with some reflections on how we manage our private finances. Few of us would sit down once a year and decide in detail exactly how much to spend on what for the coming year. We know our expected income level and our financial constraints. If the car breaks down in April, we might need to tighten other spending for a period. If we should win some money in a lottery, there is room for somewhat more. We are careful because it is our own money we spend. This is an adaptive and cost-conscious mindset, maybe the most effective cost control mechanism there is.

What if we could bring some of the same mindset with us when we go to work in the morning and start spending company money? Of course, there are differences between the two, but we should again not underestimate the importance of personal frugality.

Traditional cost budgeting does not encourage such a cost-conscious mindset. Take cost budget negotiations, where it is all about resource hoarding, securing the highest budget possible. Once approved, "entitlement" kicks in. It is now "my money". When spending decisions are made, the main question is "Do I have a budget for this?" Toward year-end, it is about "How much is left?" It is such a silly game.

The questions we need to hear instead, all the time, are very different. "Is this the right thing to do?" "How much value will this create?" "Can we afford this as things look today?" Again, processes drive behaviors, thinking, and questions asked.

We also need to get out of a "too early and too detailed" pre-allocation of resources. The more we *pre-allocate*, and the more detailed, the higher the need to *re-allocate* when things change, triggering even more negotiations and bureaucracy. We do, of course, make resource allocation assumptions when we plan and forecast, but these are not final decisions and commitments.

We also need to leave behind a myopic focus on low cost in favor of a more value-oriented thinking. There are both "good" and "bad" costs. Good costs create value, and bad costs don't. If we can fund it, we want as much good cost as possible. When a former Equinor CFO was asked by employees about the difference between the two, his response was "You guys know the answer even better than I do."

Marcin Floryan, technology operations lead at Spotify, put it like this: "Spending is fine, wasting is not," He spent several years working for a more traditional company before joining Spotify. When he started, he needed a new keyboard. When asking his manager about how to order it, he was shown a cupboard full of equipment. "Just take one" was the message. "But who approves?" he asked, noting that all equipment had a price tag. "No one. And the price tag is there to help you make informed decisions."

We also need to change the rhythm of decision-making on costs. As previously discussed, the later we can make our decisions, the better information we have, not just about what we shall say "yes" or "no" to but also if we can afford it or not.

Finally, we must move decisions closer to those who have the best information, which means more autonomy compared to what traditional budgeting advocates.

To sum it up, the Beyond Budgeting way of managing cost is about making cost decisions at *the right time, at the right level, and for the right reasons.*

Let me make it all more concrete. It is useful to separate projects (mainly, but not limited to, investment projects) and operating costs because the mechanisms will often be different.

Let us start with investment projects. Here is an example of how Equinor handles investment project approvals. This is a capital intensive business; the company invests between $10 billion and $15 billion annually. Although there have been some self-imposed overall constraints in place recently, there is no annual, detailed investment budget with all decisions being made once a year.

Instead, "the bank is always open." Anyone can forward projects for approval at any time. How high up one needs to go is regulated by a decision authority structure, which needs to be generous enough to make sure decisions are made at the right level.

"Yes" or "no" to a project depends on the answers to two questions: How good is the project—strategically, financially, and non-financially? Is there financial capacity, as things look today? This question is answered by checking the latest forecast.

Project approval means that resources are now allocated to the project. For multiyear projects this means the entire project, not just the first year.

The budget purpose separation is also applied here. Instead of a single project budget number of, say, 100, there are now three numbers. One hundred is now the initial cost *forecast*, the number used in the business case. This will start to move the moment the project starts. Because 100 represents the expected outcome, the likelihood of ending above is just as high as ending below. To avoid that, on average, every second project must come back and ask for more money; there is also a more robust *resource allocation* amount of, say, 105. There is no need for formally asking for more before the forecast exceeds this number. Finally, there is a more ambitious *target* of, for instance, 95.

Let us now move to operating costs. Although these seldom have the same distinct and formal business case decision points, it is still about making sound decisions within a clear but dynamic execution framework.

Imagine a business requiring fuel to operate. What would be best for this business: to receive an annual delivery of a fixed number of fuel cans or have a pipeline access, where the total fuel consumed depends on how much is produced?

Here is a menu of alternative mechanisms that can be used to manage operating costs, as also illustrated in Figure 4.2.

- Burn rate guiding ("Operate with full autonomy within this overall number.")
- Unit cost constraints ("You can spend more if you produce or sell more.")
- Benchmark constraints ("Your unit cost should be below the average of peers.")
- Bottom line focus only ("You can spend more if your bottom line improves even more.")
- Monitoring only ("We'll monitor actual cost trends and intervene only if needed.")

Support functions would typically apply "burn rate guiding" or "monitoring only," whereas the other alternatives are better suited for operating or commercial units, even if these still can use the full menu.

The tools described should be supplemented with a decision authority structure, as discussed previously. In addition, *guidelines* can also be put in place, such as, for instance, when to fly business versus economy. This guides local decision-making but says nothing about the level of travel cost.

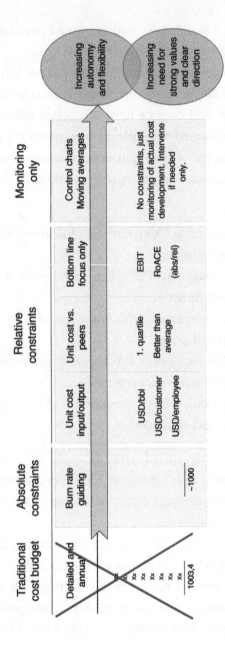

Figure 4.2 Tools for cost management.

Traditional cost budget	Absolute constraints	Unit cost input/output	Relative constraints Unit cost vs. peers	Bottom line focus only	Monitoring only
Detailed and annual	Burn rate guiding	USD/bbl USD/customer USD/employee	1. quartile Better than average	EBIT RoACE (abs/rel)	Control charts Moving averages
xx xx xx xx xx 1003,4	~1000				No constraints, just monitoring of actual cost development. Intervene if needed only.

Increasing autonomy and flexibility

Increasing need for strong values and clear direction

Supported by decision authorities and spending guidelines

This Is Beyond Budgeting

These constraints must be generous enough to reflect corresponding leadership messages about trust, empowerment, and autonomy.

Control charts and moving average totals (MATs), which we will discuss later, are good ways of monitoring cost trends.

How to fund agile teams is something we often are asked about. The first and maybe the most important resource allocation decision is, of course, about the size of it when an agile team is established. People cost is by far the largest cost category here. As the team goes to work resource allocation also here typically falls into two categories. For ongoing development work the size of the team represents an overall burn rate that needs to be optimized in the best possible way. For major new activities, maybe with a larger portion of external cost (e.g., new software licenses or external support), with distinct "yes"/"no" decision points, then the "bank is always open" approach can be applied. Funds can also be released incrementally when major milestones are reached.

The further to the right we move on the alternatives in Figure 4.2, the more trust is shown, and the more likely that someone will abuse it, consciously or unconsciously. But this is not the issue. It is how we respond.

The simple but wrong response is to punish everyone by reverting to detailed budget management because someone broke the trust. The right response, which takes more leadership, is to deal firmly with those involved and let it have the necessary consequences. Beyond Budgeting is not about being soft and evasive.

My work has involved a lot of traveling. The first thing I check when entering a hotel room is what kind of clothing hangers they have. Do they come with a hook for the rail, or are they the hopeless type without? I believe we all can agree that the second type is a hassle to use compared to the first one. So how come so many hotels offer their guests something so inconvenient? We all know why. It is about a few stolen hook hangers. And the response? Punish everybody because somebody did something wrong.

A final reflection on trust. How much we trust seems to depend on how much we understand what we trust. A friend of mine was a captain with a large international airline. Every time he was in the air, he was trusted with the responsibility for hundreds of people's lives, and some quite expensive planes as well. But a change of uniform shirt more often than regulated in the uniform procedure required a written approval from the level above.

Performance Measurement and Evaluation

Measurement can provide good input for a performance evaluation, so let us start with a few alternatives to traditional measurement methods.

Control charts can be an effective way of monitoring trends. Based on a period of historical data, a control chart provides the average of these and also upper and lower control limits. When we start reporting, new monthly actuals above or below average can be ignored if they are within these limits. It is only noise or natural variation. Readings above or below these limits, however, should be investigated. These are signals, not noise. This approach eliminates a lot of waste in analysis work.

MATs are also a good way of monitoring trends. A MAT is the sum of the last 12 months, changing monthly when data for the new month are added and data for the first month are taken away. A MAT smoothens trends and eliminates the impact of seasonal effects when plotted on a graph. By comparing the month added with the month taken away we can easily see what is driving trends. It gives us a better picture of what is happening.

Budget variance analysis is key in a budget world, comparing actual year to date numbers with corresponding budget numbers and then explaining variances. Many ask, "If there is no budget, what shall we then compare against?" as if comparing is a goal in itself. Traditional variance analysis between actual and budget numbers can't be done anymore because the budget is gone. Comparison with similar older actual numbers, for instance, can, of course, be done and often makes sense.

We should not replace budget variance analysis with a similar backwards-looking target variance analysis. What we should do is to look forward and compare *forecasts with targets*. If we don't like what we see, what do we need to do? If it looks OK, what kind of risks can jeopardize what we believe lies ahead, and how can we mitigate these risks?

Such a comparison, of course, is more difficult with relative targets as we typically can't forecast how peers will perform.

Performance evaluation must never be reduced to just a numbers exercise. Beyond Budgeting recommends a holistic performance evaluation. Let us explore why.

Targets are often expressed through KPIs. When we convert everything into three-letter acronyms, we often forget what the letters stand for. Many seem to have forgotten that the *I* in KPI stands for "indicator." A KPI indicates whether we are moving in the right direction. The indication can be strong or weak, but it seldom tells us the full truth. It is not called a KPT: key performance truth!

We therefore need to look behind measured indications before any conclusions can be drawn. Do not forget these wise words: "Not everything that counts can be counted, and not everything that can be counted counts" (No, it wasn't Albert Einstein, but William Bruce Cameron). We therefore need a holistic performance evaluation. Focusing blindly on measurement and targets can be highly problematic, even when there is no uncertainty or change in assumptions. We have seen too many sad examples of blind KPI management running the show, with disastrous results. If you can't manage what you can't measure, you have a serious problem.

If we do set KPI targets, we must consider the following:

- Indicator uncertainty. How well does the KPI measure performance? How big is the *I*, that is, how weak or strong is the indication?
- Target uncertainty. What is the right target number on the KPI?

There are also other questions that should be asked in a holistic performance evaluation, where we pressure test measured performance: How did we achieve our results? How ambitious were the targets? Was there a headwind or tailwind? Which risks were taken? How sustainable are the results?

Some argue that such assessments make the performance evaluation too subjective. They prefer the assumed objectivity of comparing only measured results to targets, end of story. But as discussed, this objectivity is an illusion due to the subjectivity going into target setting in the first place (KPI choice and target level). This longing for full objectivity might also have something to do with managerial laziness. It is much easier to compare just two numbers. Making a deeper performance assessment by looking at what really happened, digging behind measured results to reveal the true underlying performance, requires more effort. Some find this cumbersome, even difficult. But we need leaders with competence beyond the ability to count and compare. Leadership is not meant to be easy.

The most important principle in Equinor goes like this: "How we deliver is as important as what we deliver." *How* is defined by the Equinor values, and *what* by Ambition to Action directly for teams who have one, or indirectly through a translation of the nearest one into own delivery goals. The weighting between the two is 50/50, affecting both pay and career. It goes without saying that such a performance evaluation is about much more than comparing numbers.

Separate and Improve

I recall when this principle was introduced at Equinor. Some called it a brave decision because only a few organizations have done this. I would rather call it an obvious decision. How can anyone claim to be a values-based organization if values are completely absent in their performance process?

*****

Ambition to Action translates strategy into the following:

- Strategic objectives ("Where are we going? What does success look like?")
- Risks ("What are the risk we need to address?")
- Actions ("What would take us toward strategic objectives and/or mitigate risks?")
- Indicators ("How do we measure progress?")

This is done in five areas (perspectives): Safety, security and sustainability; People and organization; Operations, Market, and Finance, inspired by the balanced scorecard concept.

Equinor has about 900 Ambition to Actions throughout the organization, all aligned and connected by units translating directions and ambition levels expressed above into their own Ambition to Action. With a few exceptions there is full transparency to stimulate learning and provide control. The updating rhythm is more event driven than calendar driven.

For more about Ambition to Action, check out my previous books.

Rewards

As you will have seen from the principles, Beyond Budgeting recommends common bonus schemes instead of individual ones, preferably driven by company performance versus competition, for several reasons.

Think about it. How individual is performance really in organizations today? Isn't there always someone next to us or behind us when we deliver? This even goes for sales, which many regard as the ultimate Lone Ranger job. Maybe that great deal today had something to do with great back office work on the previous deal? We seem to have forgotten that *company* comes from *companio*, or *companion*. *Together*.

Individual bonus schemes are typically justified with two arguments that are not related but often mixed.

The first is a *market* argument: "We must be attractive as employers." I accept this, but there are many ways of being attractive. Handelsbanken has no problems with recruiting and retaining great people without offering individual bonuses. This is the case even in the UK, where for many years it was the fastest growing bank and thus needed a lot of new people, including managers recruited from competitors with hefty individual bonus schemes. You will hear from one of these managers later.

The second argument is quite different: "Individual bonuses are necessary for *motivating* people." This is where the myth kicks in. I can hardly think of a larger gap between what so many organizations practice and what so much research tells us. Individual bonuses can be highly effective under the following circumstances: if there is little motivation in the job itself, if measuring is easy, and if quantity is more important than quality. So, for picking carrots, catching rats, simple sales work (well . . .), and similar jobs, the external or extrinsic motivation of individual bonus does lead to better performance.

But when we move to more complex and team-based knowledge work, money loses its motivating power to mastery, autonomy, purpose, and belonging; the joy of getting better at something, the trust experienced when not being micromanaged, the feeling of being part of something big and noble, and the importance of teamwork and togetherness. These internal or intrinsic motivators are all more powerful than a bag of money in front of your nose. What these have in common (beyond the fact that they all come for free) is *leadership*, which, of course, is more demanding than dangling carrots in front of people. I can't help but think that the individual bonus is also about managerial laziness.

Most would accept the existence of both intrinsic and extrinsic motivation. What if we add a dose of extrinsic motivation, like an individual bonus, on top of the intrinsic motivation? Wouldn't that increase total motivation?

Most research tells a different story. The combination has either no effect at all or a negative one. Why? Because "Do this and get that" diminishes work, and shifts focus from task to reward. The implicit, and probably unintended, message is that the job you are asked to do is not interesting enough to fully motivate you.

I have been on individual bonus schemes for most of my career. Of course, I enjoyed the money, but if someone believed this was what motivated me, they had not done their homework. I am not saying money is not important, but Alfie Kohn's wise words about a decent base pay resonate with me. "Pay people fairly and get money off the table."

I am optimistic, though. There are positive signs. Some years ago, the Nordic insurance giant If abolished individual bonuses in their customer center in favor of a shared bonus scheme and somewhat higher base salaries. The result? Better employee and customer satisfaction and improved business performance.

Liechtenstein-based Hilti, selling construction products and services in 120 countries, abolished individual bonuses for almost 200 of its salespeople in Eastern Europe. The results were amazing. The affected units outperformed the market with 40%, twice as much as the year before. Staff turnover fell, and the satisfaction with pay increased almost 20%. Given the very positive results, Hilti is now considering how to best introduce the principles more broadly in the company.

Recently, Maersk Tankers followed other companies in the huge Danish Maersk Group in abolishing individual bonuses, replacing them with a common incentive system. Their motivation: to recruit and retain people who value cooperation and common results more than a focus on individual heroes.

Another Danish organization, the office supplies business Kontor Syd, dropped both bonuses and budgets a few years back, and recently posted record profits.

The Boston/Seoul-based biotech company Orum Therapeutics has no individual bonuses but a common scheme based on a set of company-wide goals. In addition, employees vote once a year on who in the company they feel makes the biggest difference. Each employee gets 100 votes to distribute to other colleagues. The more votes an employee receives, the higher the number of stock options granted. According to the company's CEO, the results are very well in line with management's own evaluations.

As we soon will learn more about, Handelsbanken has operated without individual bonuses since 1970 with amazing results.

Even management consultant firms seem to be waking up. It began with recommending their clients to move away from traditional performance ratings and make the link to pay more based on assessments. Several of them have now done this themselves (they don't always follow their own advice . . .). Some have also moved toward more common bonus schemes, a sign I hope will soon result in a strong and unified message from this powerful part of the business world: Individual bonus is incompatible not just with what research is telling us. It is also very much in conflict with the spirit of Lean and Agile, which these firms often help their clients implement. The focus on team, flow, and customers in these concepts is the very opposite of what results from "do this and get that."

Here are more wise words from Dee Hock: "Money motivates neither the best people, nor the best in people."

Key Takeaways

- Beyond Budgeting recommends relative targets where possible, both external and internal, versus competition and between teams. Such targets are self-regulating and robust against changes in assumptions because these typically apply to all. They stimulate learning, especially if they get some help from the reward system. They can also be evergreen, lasting much longer than just a year.
- Going Beyond Budgeting does, however, not depend on relative targets. Absolute targets can also be used, but these increase the need for a holistic performance evaluation.
- What we really are after is not hitting a certain number, but the best possible performance, given the circumstances. The most progressive Beyond Budgeting organizations operates without targets.
- Beyond Budgeting forecasting recommendations include required behavior changes for those on the receiving end of "good forecasts with bad news" and process recommendations on forecasting rhythm and horizons, granularity, bucket sizes, quality measurement, and how to best apply forecasts in reporting.

- Beyond Budgeting recommends that cost decisions are made at the right time (as late as possible), at the right level (as close as possible to those with the best information), and for the right reason (the best value creation).

- It is useful to separate between projects with distinct decision points and running operational or administrative activities. For projects, make sure "the bank is always open." For running costs, options include burn rate guiding, unit cost targets, benchmarked unit cost targets, bottom line targets, or only cost monitoring. Nurturing a cost-conscious mindset is key, inspired by how most of us handle our private money.

- Control charts and MATs are good measurement and evaluation tools, focusing on understanding actual performance instead of budget variances.

- Performance evaluation must never be reduced to being about hitting budget targets only. Major headwind/tailwind and other new information must be considered in a holistic evaluation. KPIs are not KPTs.

- Common bonus schemes are way better than individual ones. Still, this is not a showstopper. If there is no way around individual bonuses, the damage they cause can be reduced by applying Beyond Budgeting recommendations on how bonus targets are set and how performance is measured and evaluated. A holistic performance evaluation is even more important with individual bonuses around.

Chapter 5

Beyond Budgeting for Whom?

Beyond Budgeting for Small and Big

Most organizations are born Beyond Budgeting. They are nimble, trusting, collaborative, non-bureaucratic, and purpose driven. But few want to remain small. Most want to grow and become big. Those who make it have often something in common. They discover that they have not only become big, but they also have become slow, rigid, bureaucratic, detached, and often quite sad places to work. Engagement has plummeted, employee turnover increased, and customers are groaning. Consciously or unconsciously, they drifted away from what they used to be.

There are some striking similarities with the aging process of humans. As we get older, we lose much of the agility we had as teenagers. Mostly physically, but something tends to happen upstairs as well. This development in our body and mind is unavoidable. We can live healthily, but in the end, age takes us all. We have no choice.

Organizations, however, have a choice. There is no natural law stating that big must mean slow and sad. An increasing number of executive teams are therefore asking themselves important questions: "How can we find our way back to what we had being small, without losing the benefit of being big? How can we be big and small at the same time?"

Likewise, small organizations wanting to grow should ask themselves something few do: "How can we grow without ending up in the same misery?" It is possible, but only if you are highly conscious about it.

Beyond Budgeting can help both: those wanting to stay true to their start-up spirit and those who didn't, but regret and look for a way back. It is, however, always more challenging to remove "stupid stuff" than not to implement it in the first place.

Beyond Budgeting for Improvers and Transformers

We know that people perceive Beyond Budgeting in different ways, depending on how they heard about it, the roles they are in, and the implementation experiences they may have had. Some see implementation merely as an improvement of finance processes, while we and many others see it also as a model capable of creating a much broader organizational transformation.

We should, however, be careful with labeling implementation approaches as either right or wrong, for at least two reasons.

First, it is better to do something than nothing at all. There are, for instance, many benefits in separating target setting, forecasting, and resource allocation, even if there still are absolute numbers and calendar rhythms, and leadership isn't addressed.

Second, most get braver along the way. What was scary yesterday is often no longer scary today because it worked. Bravery might one day take organizations toward a broader transformation, even if this wasn't the original intention.

At least for now, I believe we must accept that most implementation cases will not start out as full-blown transformations. This does not diminish Beyond Budgeting and what the model aims for. Without further comparison, it must be better to live by five of the ten amendments than none of them.

Even if the ambition is limited to only improving finance processes, it is still important to understand the full model and the philosophy behind. This will help and guide process design, and make sure that initial solutions allow for and do not block a longer journey if the time comes. A good understanding might also increase the appetite for a broader transformation.

Beyond Budgeting is for both improvers and transformers. Many in the first category will end up in the second. I do believe this distinction will disappear one day as it becomes obvious for all that the only way is transformation.

We have developed a map and a method to help organizations better understand where they are, where they want to be, and how to get there on the journey from improver to transformer. The Viable Map is described in Chapter 8.

Can Beyond Budgeting Work in the Public Sector?

Let me start with the answer to this question. It is a clear "yes." Not only can it work. The public sector needs Beyond Budgeting just as much as its private counterpart.

There are many reasons why the question keeps being raised, and why most believe the answer is no.

Today, the public sector suffers from much of the same management problems that the private sector has struggled with for decades. It has ended up in the same misery because it blindly copied beliefs and thinking from private sector management. The "new public management" concept, which started out in the United Kingdom and Australia, has today spread across the Western world. Even progressive Scandinavia hasn't been immune to these ideas, which are heavily inspired by business thinking about targets, measurement, markets, and contracts.

The irony is that this happened at the same time as the private sector was starting to realize that its traditional management beliefs and practices didn't work that well. New public management was born in the 1990s, in the same decade as Beyond Budgeting, but the two represent very different philosophies.

Maybe the public sector needs this sad detour into management and leadership wilderness to fully understand how dysfunctional it is. Maybe it increases the appetite for something different and better.

So why do so many believe that Beyond Budgeting can't work in the public sector? It starts, of course, with the name, which draws attention to the budget word and to the public funding regime of annual budgets. But even if there is an annual process, a big bag of money from above once a year, why must we immediately turn around and split this bag into thousands of smaller bags handed out as next year's detailed budget for every cost category and for every tiniest box on the organization chart?

Why not instead treat this overall funding as a constraint, something we need to optimize within as effectively as possible? This means pre-allocating at little as possible and instead making cost decisions more continuously, at the right time, at the right level, and for the right reasons. This is just as relevant and important here as in the private sector.

Even if many of the dynamic resource allocation mechanisms in Beyond Budgeting were developed with private companies in mind, some would work just as well in the public sector. Take for instance "burn rate guiding," which as you will recall means "operate at an activity level that expressed in money is in the range of x, until something else is decided." No micromanagement, no travel or consultant budgets.

The "monitoring only" alternative can also work. No budget, no pre-allocation, just a monitoring of cost trends with intervention only when unacceptable trends are observed. Even relative targets can work, if applied in a Beyond Budgeting and not in a new public management context. The "decision authorities" and "guidelines" mechanisms are also just as relevant here and are probably in place already.

In 2020, the contact center in the Norwegian social services organization NAV tested the "monitoring only" alternative. Two of 12 units across the country were allowed to operate without a cost budget for administrative cost, although hiring still required approval. The message was simple. Spend what is needed to do a good job, and not more. The results were amazing. As the experiment took place during the pandemic, all centers had lower external activities and costs that year, but no one had higher cost reductions than the two pilots. Minus 50% in both! The experiment was extended to six units in 2021, and from 2022 all 12 operate without traditional costs budgets.

All the other Beyond Budgeting principles should also be just as relevant in the public sector. Don't tell me that purpose, values, and transparency are less needed here. The same goes for internal relative targets, rolling forecasts, and a holistic performance evaluation. Although less prevalent, individual bonus does just as much damage here as in the private sector.

The Dutch home care organization Buurtzorg has for many years provided solid evidence that public services can be delivered in much more human and effective ways than what new public management offers. The world has started to notice, and many home care institutions have adopted a similar model. A few failed, mainly because they just copied the structure but not the philosophy behind it.

Companies on the Journey

We are often asked "Who is doing this?" Figure 5.1 provides an overview of companies we know are on a Beyond Budgeting journey in some form or shape. There are certainly more, which we haven't heard of or helped. There are probably also companies operating in line with the model without even having heard of Beyond Budgeting.

Some of the companies here started out many years ago, others more recently. There are both improvers and transformers. Some have been cautious and stepwise in their approach. Others have been extremely radical from day one. Most are somewhere in between. They have all, however, kicked out the traditional, detailed, annual budget. What varies is what they have done instead and how much their new management processes are inspired by Beyond Budgeting leadership principles on purpose, values, autonomy, and transparency. What most have in common is that they got braver along the way and that they tend to perform well among peers.

Most of these companies are based in Europe, many in the US, and some in other parts of the world. Many of them operate transnationally. Silicon Valley is surprisingly absent. Our experience is that although these companies are vanguards on technology innovation, many are laggards on management innovation. Maybe upcoming IPOs (being listed on the stock exchange) required recruiting CFOs with their mind on very different issues than the company's management model.

Figure 5.1 Companies on the journey.
Source: Beyond Budgeting Institute.

This Is Beyond Budgeting

You won't find Borealis here. The company had a major shift in ownership, including Equinor pulling out, resulting in a new management team, quite cold on Beyond Budgeting. I am still proud of what we did, how we inspired Beyond Budgeting, and how our model helped other companies getting started.

I believe there are three reasons why European companies so far are dominating:

- Beyond Budgeting is a European invention, unlike most other management concepts, which were invented in the US (the balanced scorecard, OKRs, and budgets. . .).
- The Beyond Budgeting Roundtable is currently present only in Europe and has therefore focused its activities here.
- The European, and especially the Nordic, culture is probably closer to the spirit of Beyond Budgeting than for instance US or Asian cultures, which tend to be more hierarchical and control oriented.

Many regards cultural differences as a showstopper. I disagree. What we label cultural challenges are sometimes only about being stuck in traditional management thinking, something managers across the world struggle with.

Even when there are cultural issues, most of the management process recommendations are just as relevant, such as a more event-driven rhythm, relative targets, rolling forecasts, a more dynamic resource allocation, and a holistic performance evaluation. The Beyond Budgeting criticism of individual bonuses is very much in line with the more collective focus found in many Asian cultures.

It is also important to note that very few go back to the old way once they have started. What the few who did have in common was either an early and major change in top management or a flawed implementation, typically not building a solid enough case for change or implementing rolling forecasts only. More about this later.

There are so many great stories to be told about the companies shown in Figure 5.1. Handelsbanken is an amazing case that I will come back to. My first books told the story about the Norwegian company Miles. I encourage you to check out this fascinating company, a master in servant leadership, with no budgets or targets.

The fastest implementation I so far have been involved with was for David Lloyd Leisure, a leading health, sport, and leisure provider with 126 clubs across the United Kingdom and continental Europe. I had my first session with the company in October 2019. By January 1 they were up and running, making the organization much more resilient and adaptive when the pandemic hit some months later. The company weathered the crisis and is today performing extremely well.

David Lloyd Leisure is owned by TDR Capital, a UK-based private equity firm. TDR's philosophy is to invest in "undermanaged" companies and improve their performance and value by helping them improve their management model. TDR is looking at Beyond Budgeting as a model that resonates well with what TDR regards as good management.

We also helped another of its companies, Hurtigruten, an expedition travel and cruise company, get started before the pandemic hit. We are now back again, working with several other of their companies.

Years ago, few had heard about Chinese Haier. Today this is the world's largest whitegoods producer with 100,000 employees, many outside China.

The former CEO Zhang Ruimin, now retired, has a keen interest in management innovation. He used the knowledge he acquired not just to copy what he read, but to develop Haier into one of the most innovatively managed companies in the world.

Some years ago, he came across Beyond Budgeting and my second book, and I was invited over to Haier's headquarters in Qingdao. To prepare myself, I read a book about the company's unique management model on the way over. The meeting started, and I asked a question based on what I had read. Ruimin smiled and said, "That was two years ago." The company has such an amazing speed on its management innovation. It is inspired by the organization of the internet, which has no central power but billions of local nodes. The company has organized itself in thousands of small autonomous micro enterprises, often with employee ownership. These can deal with each other and with the outside world more or less as they wish.

I had an ambition of writing a case story about Haier, but I still haven't got my head fully around all aspects of their amazing model. But now the job is done. Check out *Harvard*

Business Review's 2018 article "The End of Bureaucracy" by Gary Hamel and Michele Zanini and also their book *Humanocracy*.

Most of the companies I work with are larger ones. Their challenge is to throw out legacy management models. As mentioned, it is always more difficult to get rid of "stupid stuff" than not to implement it in the first place. It often seems so obvious to implement what everybody else is doing rather than to go your own way. Miles and others have shown us that it is possible.

I have worked with several organizations in this category, including the already mentioned Orum Therapeutics. I always start out trying to understand which problems the company is trying to solve. The CEO was very clear. "This isn't about solving problems we have today, but about avoiding those we will get if we unconsciously drift into them as we grow." Wise words from a wise man.

Key Takeaways

- Most organizations are born Beyond Budgeting but lose it as they grow and unconsciously drift toward becoming rigid, bureaucratic, and sad places to work. It is always more difficult to get rid of "stupid stuff" than not to implement it in the first place.
- Beyond Budgeting can be about improving finance processes, or transforming organizations, or any-

---

thing in between. Very few go back, and most get braver along the way.

- Beyond Budgeting is just as relevant and just as needed in the public as in the private sector. New public management has done serious damage to this important sector.
- Organizations all over the world have embarked on Beyond Budgeting journeys. Most of them are in Europe, many in the US but there are also many exciting cases in other parts of the world.

Chapter 6

Agile Transformation

M any large organizations are today on an agile transformation journey in some form or shape. Although there are many similarities between the Beyond Budgeting principles and the Agile Manifesto, there are also some important differences. Due to its birthplace in software development and its focus on how teams work, a range of corporate management issues were left out of scope for early agile, for instance, budgeting. Beyond Budgeting, on the contrary, was born as a challenge to traditional corporate management, and therefore it addresses the many issues early agile didn't need to.

Transformation is, by the way, a word I struggle with, even if I have used it several times. It indicates a project with an end date. An agile transformation, or a Beyond Budgeting implementation, is not a project. It is a journey where the direction is clearer than the destination, if there is one.

In this chapter, we will also discuss OKRs and psychological safety, concepts that also fit well with Beyond Budgeting and that especially the agile community has embraced.

The Elephant in the Room

When agile was born, it was not about big organizations asking big questions about reinventing themselves as the start-ups many of them used to be. Although agile was rebelling against many aspects of traditional management, the focus was on how it negatively affected software development and how teams worked, not on how entire organizations should operate in agile ways.

Agile challenged waterfall planning, business case documentation, economy of scale, almighty managers managing siloed work, and many other traditional management beliefs. A vibrant agile community and great new ways of working emerged, all inspired by the Agile Manifesto.

And here we are, many years later. The results are simply amazing. Agile has revolutionized software development and related teamwork practices and has also been successfully applied in start-ups.

It has become the new standard. It is non-controversial. Nobody is discussing going back; it is all about making agile work even better.

Scaling agile, which later developed into various business agility frameworks, was therefore a natural development based on the strong belief that the entire organization needs to operate on agile principles. This came, however, with a few caveats. The fact that IT functions embraced agile did not solve the many fundamental conflicts between traditional corporate processes and the agile philosophy.

Beyond Budgeting was about business agility long before the term appeared. It is the missing link in many agile transformations, and if left unaddressed, transformation success is highly unlikely. Beyond Budgeting also provides a business agility vocabulary that executives understand, even if some disagree.

The initial success of agile has much to do with its birthplace. What executives in large organizations observed in those early years was faster and better projects and more engaged employees. Who can be against this? But when agile scaled and started to challenge executive beliefs and behaviors, it wasn't that fun anymore. Just like what happened with many of the attempts to scale Lean.

It is also hard to scale agile using the same frameworks and language that served early "software and team" agile so well. *Scrum* might sound like a skin disease for executives unfamiliar with agile or rugby. *Sprints* are not about running faster. *Slack* is not about laziness. *Continuous delivery* is not about 24/7 or faster assembly lines.

We therefore need a translation, something that can help executive teams better understand what agile means at a corporate level. What does business agility really mean in practice?

But there is an elephant in the room, a problem agile has been suffering from since its early days. Although there have been complaints, little has happened. Maybe because the annual budget was seen as something given, a law of business, unavoidable and untouchable.

As you now will know, this is all wrong. There is no such law, and if this elephant isn't addressed, any agile transformation will struggle.

Traditional budgeting is probably the most fundamental barrier there is to an agile transformation. Not just the annual budget and the budgeting process itself, but just as much the mindset behind it: people can't be trusted, the future is predictable. These assumptions are the antithesis of agile. It doesn't get more unagile.

The agile principle of continuous delivery of software functionality instead of big batch releases is a classic example of philosophy crash. An annual cost budget is a big batch of decisions and resources and not a continuous delivery of funds as needs appears.

Maybe it was no coincidence that Beyond Budgeting and agile were born roughly at the same time (Beyond Budgeting is slightly older), and that the 12 Beyond Budgeting principles have so much in common with the Agile Manifesto, even if there was no contact between the two communities back then. Or make that almost no contact. According to the Agile Alliance, "XP2000, held in June 2000 on the Mediterranean island of Sardinia with over 100 attendees, was the first Agile conference worldwide." I was there, sharing Beyond Budgeting with a great group of people. This was even before the Agile Manifesto had been developed.

I have been a fan of agile since its early days. It has over the years done wonders for many organizations. I have, however, a recommendation and a few concerns. The Agile Manifesto needs an update. Although it has been surprisingly robust, given its birthplace, the concept is now applied way outside of its original scope. An update reflecting this would make the Manifesto more relevant and easier to understand and implement for the many without a background in software development.

Now to my concerns. Lately, we have seen the emergence of an agile industry. I see so many actors in the community turning into commercial machines. Some even seem to enter only with this purpose in mind. Certification has become big business. It provokes me when I hear about expensive re-certifications being required every year.

Beyond Budgeting never joined this certification circus. How can we certify that someone gets it? We can help people understand, but we can never certify. We probably denied ourselves a nice revenue stream, but it has been worth it.

Some scaled agile implementation frameworks do, unfortunately, seem to have been developed simply to be acceptable to organizations that want to pretend they are agile but maintain top-down decision-making hierarchies. *Agile theatre* is a label I often hear, and I understand why.

Let me close with a big thank you to some of my friends in the agile community. Several years ago, I was invited to join "Supporting Agile Adoption," a group established by the Agile Alliance in 2010. Its purpose is to support both the adoption and further development of agile. The group was initially founded by Esther Derby and Diana Larsen, and was later led by Jorgen Hesselberg. I have enjoyed how the group has continued to evolve under its current leader, Hendrik Esser. Today, members include Hendrik and Jorgen, as well as Diana Larsen, Jutta Eckstein, Marcin Floryan, John Buck, Eric Abelen, Jens Coldewey, Claudia Meo, and me. Ray Arell, Esther Derby, Don Gray, and many others also participated for several years.

Beyond Budgeting and OKRs

Over the last few years, we have witnessed an amazing revival of an almost 50-year-old management idea: objectives and key results (OKR).

The former Intel CEO Andy Grove introduced the concept in this company in the 1970s, as described in his 1983 book *High Output Management.* John Doerr, a former Intel employee, later introduced it to a start-up called Google.

Although Google and several others, mainly Silicon Valley companies, have applied OKRs for many years, it was Doerr's 2018 book *Measure What Matters* that turbocharged the concept. OKRs are now on everybody's lips, especially in the agile community.

An OKR has two components:

- An objective, a goal—something we want to achieve
- Key results—three to five clearly defined metrics with targets and actions to achieve these

There are many aspects of OKRs that fit well with Beyond Budgeting:

- Ambitious targets. Targets should be so ambitious that meeting them is the exception, not the rule, although commitments involving customers should always be met. Beyond Budgeting also recommends ambitious targets, although we advocate relative targets when possible.

- No link to bonus is a very positive feature, as already discussed.
- OKRs are translated throughout the organization, without top-down cascading. This secures involvement and ownership.
- OKRs are open and visible for everyone, again well in line with the transparency principle in Beyond Budgeting.
- OKRs do not operate on a traditional annual rhythm, although a fixed quarterly cadence also has some issues, as discussed following.

There are, however, a few other aspects that from a Beyond Budgeting perspective are more problematic.

The assumption that everything can and must be measured is an issue. The metric part of a key result is very much a KPI, even if that term isn't used. As discussed, the *I* in KPI stands for "indicator." They only provide indications. Also, not everything can be measured.

Although key result targets are set by teams themselves, target setting can still be problematic. If there is uncertainty, how do we know what the right number is? It does, of course, help that the time horizon is relatively short.

No judgment in the performance evaluation is especially toxic. "The key result has to be measurable. At the end you can look, and without any arguments: Did I do it or did I not do it? Yes? No? Simple. No judgments in it," Doerr writes. Although he might be talking more about action completion than measured results against targets, there seems to be an assumption that judgment is wrong. Beyond Budgeting disagrees. "Evaluate performance holistically. . . , not based on measurement only. . . ."

A quarterly rhythm is usually much better than an annual one. However, it is still a fixed rhythm, which might be too frequent for some and the opposite for others.

I have not seen much in the OKR literature about budgets, probably because most companies using OKRs also have budgets and take them for granted. This is problematic, and not just for the reasons we already have discussed. There will often be conflicts between directions and messages coming from the budget and those coming from OKRs. I have experienced the same conflict between budgets and balanced scorecards. When push comes to shove, the budget always wins, sending a clear message about who runs the show and what really matters. One of many benefits of removing the budget is the strong signal it sends of being serious about what remains. OKRs can now take its place at the core of the management model.

Let me finish with a comparison of OKRs and Equinor's Ambition to Action. There are many similarities, but also some differences beyond those described.

Ambition to Action starts out with a longer-term ambition statement, which is not found in an OKR. Both have objectives, although Equinor calls them strategic objectives, with a medium-term time horizon. Ambition to Action continues with risk: the risks of not achieving these objectives or other risks coming from business activities. This is missing in an OKR.

Key results are in Ambition to Action divided in two—actions and indicators—and indicators may or may not have targets. Actions are there to take teams toward strategic objectives, or mitigate risk, or both. Indicators try to measure progress toward strategic objectives. Separating these, as Equinor did, improves in my view the quality of both.

Beyond this, there is a shared philosophy of translation, transparency, and escaping the calendar year strait jacket.

If you want to learn more about Ambition to Action, my previous books have a thorough description of the model and the process for it.

I hope you don't read this as a refutation of OKRs. It is much better having them than having nothing at all. But no concept deserves being positioned as a silver bullet, not even Beyond Budgeting. Any management model can be misused. I can easily imagine a mechanical OKR implementation being used to reinforce traditional command and control as part of the agile theatre.

A final word of warning. Watch out for OKR certification. When it arrives (maybe it has already), it is often the beginning of the end, as we have seen too many times before.

Beyond Budgeting and Psychological Safety

Psychological safety has, like OKRs, also had a recent rejuvenation. The concept is not new. Already in the 1960s the organizational researchers Edgar Schein and Warren Bennis defined it as a group phenomenon that reduces a person's anxiety about being accepted and worthwhile. Later, Deming talked about the importance of "driving out fear, so that everyone may work effectively for the company."

Just like John Doerr's 2018 book turbocharged OKRs, Amy Edmondson's book *The Fearless Organization* published the same year did the same to psychological safety, describing it as key to high performance in an organization.

Edmondson has an important message. Psychological safety makes a big difference. Although Beyond Budgeting doesn't specifically use the term, it is still very much present in the spirit of the model. The Theory Y people focus and the emphasis on purpose, values, transparency, and autonomy all build psychological safety. Still, I buy the argument that trust and psychological safety is not the same. Trust is about how we view each other, while safety is about how people think they are viewed by others. Both are still important.

Psychological safety is a part of and a prerequisite for Beyond Budgeting. I might not have dared to propose what we implemented in Borealis and Equinor without feeling safe about speaking up and challenging the old way.

Still, you can't run an organization on psychological safety alone. Although it is an important part of a good management model, it only becomes real if there is coherence with the other parts of the model.

Key Takeaways

- Born at the same time, there are many similarities between Beyond Budgeting and agile, but there is also an important difference. Agile was not designed as a way to run an organization, whereas Beyond Budgeting was.
- This makes it hard to scale agile. Beyond Budgeting can help. There can be no true agile transformation without it.
- The Agile Manifesto needs an update and also protection against an emerging agile industry.
- OKRs and Beyond Budgeting have many similarities but also a few differences. OKRs will never be fully effective unless the budget competitor is removed.
- Psychological safety and Beyond Budgeting also have much in common.

Chapter 7

Handelsbanken

We keep being asked, for good reasons, about cases and practical examples. Organizations on the journey show us that Beyond Budgeting works, and they provide inspiration and guidance.

Many ask for cases from the same kind of business as themselves. Examples from very different businesses, however, can provide just as much learning. The many problems we discussed previously are universal; they tend to be independent of what kind of organization we are in.

Most of us are not in banking, but we still have a lot to learn from Handelsbanken. My first books both had a chapter about the bank. I have learned a lot more about it since then. I have also had access to some unique internal stories. One of these is found in this chapter, in which a UK branch manager describes his job and his journey

His story is important, because almost everything written about the bank's fascinating management model is written by outsiders, including myself (except for former CEO Jan Wallander's own great books). An inside story is a great way of hopefully not only confirming our understanding, but also of learning more about what it all looks and feels like inside a branch. This story also shows us that Beyond Budgeting works just as well outside of the Nordic region in a quite different business culture. Handelsbanken UK employees are sometimes seen as more Handelsbanken than their Nordic colleagues. You have something to look forward to!

But first, here is my new take on the bank's journey and their amazing model.

How It Started

Handelsbanken has today about 500 branches and more than 11,000 employees across its home markets in Sweden, Norway, the United Kingdom, and Netherlands.

The bank's fascinating Beyond Budgeting journey started in another Swedish bank. In 1961, Sundsvallbanken appointed a young academic, Jan Wallander, as its new CEO. He knew little about banking but quickly got a good grasp of the business. More important, he saw ways of improving the bank's performance by changing how it was led and managed. In the following years, he abolished traditional budgeting, introduced relative measurement, decentralized decision-making, and stopped running central marketing campaigns. The accounting system that had been focused solely on external statutory reporting was radically improved to also provide internal branch performance information.

Profitability and market share increased. The major banks started to notice as they were losing customers to this much smaller bank.

One of these was Handelsbanken, the largest bank not just in Sweden but in the Nordic region at the time. It was formed in 1871 and is the oldest company on the Swedish stock exchange.

The bank was now in trouble and was also in conflict with regulatory authorities. In 1970, Wallander was offered the CEO role. After much hesitation, he accepted on the condition that he could continue developing what he had started in Sundsvallbanken.

The bank where it all started went through several mergers and became Nordbanken, which later, through further mergers and acquisitions developed into Nordea, today one of the 10 largest financial groups in Europe. Along the way Wallander's ideas got lost. The gravity of the old way is strong. We can only speculate about what would have happened if he had stayed on.

The Model

Wallander quickly introduced what had worked so well in Sundsvallbanken. He established a set of key principles that are just as valid today as back then. The bank's ambition is to have a higher return on equity than the average of its main competitors, achieved through lower cost and higher customer satisfaction. The focus is on value, not volume.

Branches shall have as much decision-making power as possible, and the head office shall be small. Its main purpose is to support the branches. "The branch is the bank," as they put it. The organizational structure is flat, with few levels. The organization chart used to be called the *Arrow*, everything pointing towards the customer. No one moves up or down in the organization, just closer to or further away from the customer.

Many head office and middle manager roles disappeared. No one was fired, as most were offered branch office roles. Lately, some branches have been closed because many of these were quite small; some open only a few hours a week. Most of these teams were combined into a bigger branch offering a higher level of qualified advice.

The bank's more recent digital strategy is also different from competitors, who believe it is about either being digital or local, leading to massive branch closures. Handelsbanken believes the right answer is digital *and* local. For customers, having a local contact who knows you, and you can meet in person if needed, is still important even if most of the communication happens online.

The Arrow has now evolved into a circle around the customer to reflect that customers do more and more digital business with the bank. The profit and loss and overall customer relationship (and credit) responsibility still stops with the branch, but it is no longer realistic that it can serve and represent all the customers' needs—it requires other parts of the business to take some of this customer responsibility, too (e.g., the digital and telephone banking teams). It is still very much a one-team approach, arranged around the customer.

As another result of customer behavior change and technological possibilities, the regional head offices were replaced with a country support network for the branches. Areas such as accounting, HR, and specialist support were centralized because if these were handled in several regional head offices it would subtract rather than add value; credit support was pushed closer to the branches; and advisory expertise (and credit authority) increased across the branch network. The bank became more decentralized while becoming more operationally streamlined and agile.

Wallander was very clear that the bank should not push products on customers. There is no individual bonus, only a common profit-sharing scheme. And beyond no budgets, there are no traditional targets and not much forecasting. "If you know what tomorrow will look like, why should you forecast? If you don't know, how can you?" was Wallander's simple reflection.

He also made a few small, but highly symbolic decisions. He said no to a generous salary increase and remained on the much lower renumeration level he had in his previous job. Chauffeur-driven cars were quickly phased out. He understood that culture is about what you do, not about what you say.

These principles are all described in the bank's most important document, the booklet *Our Way*. Wallander wrote the first edition. Subsequent CEOs have made smaller updates, but the spirit and the key messages are very intact.

Wallander was concerned about competitors getting hold of it, copying their model, which he knew was key to their success. It was therefore labeled strictly confidential. It had the employee's name printed and it had to be personally signed out.

Later, the bank became more open about its model, as competitors strangely enough didn't come rushing in to copy it. More about why not later.

I once asked a branch manager if I could get a copy of the booklet. The response was a polite "no". I was, however, allowed to flip through it, with the branch manager behind my back. The first words that hit my eyes were these: "We have an unshakeable belief in people and their will and ability to do things well." Wonderful words! Although they are easy to copy, the management model required to make them come alive is not.

As mentioned, the bank regards the lack of budgets as a natural consequence of their philosophy and not a goal in itself. It is just one part of the model. Coherence among all its parts is the main secret. Let us dive a bit deeper into some of these.

Although the main group financial KPI is return on equity, the main internal one for measuring branch financial performance is cost/income ratio. Because capital costs are charged to all units, there is a good correlation between the two. The bank's ambition is a higher return on equity than the average of competitors. There is, however, no cascading of this target. There is no need because there is full transparency on performance. Branches compare themselves internally, and again, no one likes to be laggards. This self-regulating mechanism also replaces cost budgets. More good cost, less bad cost, as simple as that. And who knows best the difference between the two?

Almost all credit decisions are taken locally. A "no" in a branch cannot be reversed higher up.

This Is Beyond Budgeting

Abolishing individual bonuses was not only about stimulating internal collaboration and learning, but also about customer satisfaction, as individual sales bonuses easily create a conflict of interest with customers. Have you ever wondered why your bank contact keeps asking if you need better insurance?

No individual bonuses is no longer that unique. As we have heard, an increasing number of companies are ditching these in favor of common systems. The totality of the bank's bonus system is, however, very unusual.

The common bonus, as mentioned, is driven by company performance versus competition (the idea Equinor borrowed). Many have done the same. But at Handelsbanken, everybody gets the same amount. So, who has the lowest bonus, compared to salary? The CEO! Isn't that crazy? Or maybe not. If all the research should be wrong, if an individual bonus really is needed to motivate, how come the one at the top needs the biggest dose? Should this not be among the most interesting and motivating roles there is?

The bonus is not paid out annually, only at 60 or if you leave. The bank takes a long-term perspective on everything it does and wants employees to think in the same way. This is another example of coherence throughout the management model.

Annual bonus payments are placed in *Oktogonen* (the Octagon). This foundation buys Handelsbanken shares and is now one of its largest shareholders.

The Oktogonen rules were recently adjusted because it became burdensome to comply with the various markets' tax requirements and evolving banking regulation for compensation, since the scheme operates in such an unusual way.

Every employee is still allocated the same amount. These allocations are then provided to the home markets to distribute per the most appropriate model for them. The UK, for instance, take advantage of the government's "share incentive plan" arrangement, whereby allocations sit in an account for at least 5 years (invested in Handelsbanken shares) and thereafter can be paid out to the employee tax free. The employee can, of course, keep the allocations invested beyond this point.

A common bonus scheme can also be generous. A full career in the bank has so far meant about one and a half million euros waiting at retirement.

The result of this astonishing management model is simply amazing. The bank has achieved its ambition of delivering above-average returns every year since 1972. It is among the most cost-effective universal banks in Europe and has had more satisfied customers than the industry average since surveys started in 1989. It is no coincidence that there never has been a need for a bailout from the authorities because the bank messed it up.

We should still be careful with putting the bank on a pedestal. No one is perfect. The bank has issues and challenges like everybody else. They may even fail big one day. If they should, although I very much doubt it, no one can take away what they have left behind for us.

Still, how come more banks are not trying to copy such a huge success? A few have, with impressive results. Most haven't, at least not yet.

This also goes for Nordea, the Nordic bank giant mentioned previously, even if the current CEO, Frank Vang-Jensen, is a former Handelsbanken CEO. He was appointed in 2015 and fired after only 18 months in the role. The Handelsbanken board was very explicit about why. Vang-Jensen was seen to have started to centralize power to the Stockholm headquarter. The board regards the bank's management model as so important that no CEO stands above it.

When I had finalized the Handelsbanken case story for my first book, I sent the chapter to Wallander for his comments and approval. I got a nice handwritten letter back. He liked my story and approved it, but he had one comment. I had been speculating about why more competitor CEOs were not trying to copy such an amazing success? I had forgotten the main reason. "They are afraid of losing power."

This was the second time we were in touch. The first was at a conference in Belgium many years earlier, during my Borealis days. We were both invited to speak. I came with a load of plastic slides (no PowerPoint back then!). Wallander came with a tiny piece of paper with just a few words on it. He never looked at it, and he blew us all away.

A Branch Manager's Story

When a new Handelsbanken branch is established, the manager is recruited first, who then selects the office premises. The opposite of what most other banks would do.

One of these branch managers, Alan Barnard, started his banking career in 1973 and retired just after writing this story.

In 2010, he was approached by Handelsbanken to open the new Colchester branch in the United Kingdom. Having worked for more traditional banks for many years, he is well positioned to understand and describe how radically different Handelsbanken is.

A big thank you to Alan Barnard and Robin Fraser for sharing this story. Please note that Alan wrote this before the regional level adjustment.

Over to Alan.

❈❈❈

The first decision Handelsbanken asked me to make, after recruiting me in 2010 to open the Colchester branch in southeast England, was who to recruit for my branch team. As a relationship business which relies on high service levels and solid local decisions, the qualities of the individuals brought in at the beginning would form the cornerstone and culture of our branch, its future growth, and commercial success.

I set about assembling a team of experienced and respected bankers who were all known to me, lived locally and had established business and professional networks. Between us we could boast a detailed and extensive knowledge of our Colchester 'patch', past and present, and specifically which local businesses and individuals might most value our relationship banking approach.

Now in its sixth year, our branch has already achieved record growth in terms of new business, driven very much by the advocacy of our existing customers. The team is twice the size it was three years ago and there seems no letup in demand for what we offer: traditional local relationship banking supported by all the products, services and modern channels our customers require.

Goals of my branch. The overarching goal of the branch is to achieve a sustainable 'endowment' income stream from a base of satisfied business and individual clients who themselves value long-term, local banking relationships. These clients then act as advocates, introducing additional clients, and thereby further income, to the branch.

The clarity and simplicity of both our operating model, and the culture surrounding it, is quickly recognized and appreciated by customers. They see that we are not stretching, or braking, to hit central targets, to unlock bonus incentives or to move a particular product on a particular day, week or month; they benefit from the continuity of our policies, our teams and the way that we deliver service—all of this is seen as refreshing and reassuring by our customers, who simply want the consistent attention, service and respect they deserve.

As such, it is not difficult to convince new clients who value a relationship based on trust and mutual benefit to switch to Handelsbanken. We always advise prospective customers that the reason our existing ones switched from their previous bank to us tended to have little to do with any particular product, service or price we could offer. Instead, their desire was to return to a long-remembered and cherished local banking relationship, with staff they can actually speak to and meet. The fact that we could then offer financial solutions tailored to their circumstances, as well as broader banking and wealth services, was all-but-incidental at that initial decision point.

The second goal of the branch is careful control of costs. We focus all the time to ensure our own local expenses, as well as those we are asked to cover from head office functions, are fully justified. We scrutinize contracts for suppliers large and small, since the more we can reduce costs while upholding quality of service, the more income will flow through to our branch's bottom-line profitability.

Our culture of devolved power and responsibility. The culture within Handelsbanken allows me to manage the branch with far more autonomy than I have ever seen or experienced elsewhere in the banking industry. In addition to recruitment, staff development, business growth, client selection and good administrative order, I am also ultimately responsible for all day-to-day commercial decisions made within the branch. That said, the bank's model also steers me to empower my own team with sufficient authority to take individual responsibility for providing the support and services that our clients require. This devolved responsibility helps us each to develop, as well as creating job satisfaction, eliminating inefficiencies, and of course, enabling us each to serve our customers that much more effectively.

There is nothing a customer really values more than to deal directly with someone who can make a decision in a timely manner. In terms of lending, almost all lending decisions are made within the branch, either by me or by my account managers personally who have delegated lending limits.

A simple follow-up review process, covering all lending decisions (including my own), enables individuals' discretionary limits to be increased from time to time as the branch grows, and this incremental decentralisation further improves customer service, while reducing costs.

Within the branch, other than myself there are only two other roles: account managers (corporate and individual) and account manager support. Account managers spend their time either with their clients, or analyzing and processing their requirements of us. An account manager support does exactly what their title suggests, for instance taking responsibility for physically opening accounts, preparing loan and security documentation and handling customers' everyday banking requirements.

There is no measurement of how much time anything takes. Rather there is much encouragement for staff to challenge processes and constructively suggest where changes could be made to either improve the client experience or reduce costs. (This is part of the payback the business receives from empowering its employees and providing genuine job satisfaction.)

We aim to spend as much time as possible serving our customers, speaking to them, understanding what support they need from us at that time, but also identifying where they may need support in future. One of the great benefits of this decentralized model is that we don't work in silos, and are instead able to look at a client's whole situation. Our products are designed to provide us with maximum flexibility, this means we can work closely with our customers to find the right mix of features to meet their individual requirements. We are then free to agree bespoke tariffs that reflect appropriate value to each customer.

Whenever we as a branch require specialist support, I am supported by colleagues in the bank's regional office. This might be anything from advice with complex foreign exchange trades, to discussions around unusual credit circumstances, to operational support for instance with IT or HR questions. Help is at hand whenever it is needed, although it is fair to say that the branch is very much self-sufficient for the majority of our operational needs.

My role as a manager. As a manager, I am clear about my role in guiding and supporting my team to develop an understanding of how they can best work within the bank's principles. I am not here to directly drive or manage their behaviors or force culture down my colleagues' throats.

I remember clearly when, soon after I joined the bank, the Group CEO met with a group of us newly appointed branch managers to discuss the bank's culture and our pivotal role within it. At that gathering, he said something I shall never forget, that as managers our job is not to spend a minute of our time motivating our teams. Rather, it is to ensure that we don't spend a single moment of our time de-motivating them.

This perfectly encapsulates the culture within Handelsbanken, recognizing as it does that people are naturally motivated. What, if anything, gets in the way of this is bureaucracy, targets, non-client focused activities, unnecessary internal admin tasks and—my personal pet hate from previous roles—

spending time writing reports for someone further up the pyramid to read and then present on to someone even further up. Without these unnecessary burdens and deflections, staff are left free to do what they really want to do, which is to meet the needs of our clients in the most efficient and cost-effective way.

It has sometimes been suggested that working for Handelsbanken is a lifestyle choice. And this is perhaps one aspect of the story. For instance, within six months of setting up the branch, I received a heartfelt thank you from the wife of my corporate manager for "giving the family their Dad back", after 25 years working with a British High Street bank. However, one might also consider the fact that the book of banking business this same corporate manager has developed over these past five years would be the envy of any of our local competitors, or even their regional directors.

So it is perhaps this combination of professional autonomy, personal commitment and accountability, within an all-round supportive culture, that represents the power source of our profitability.

As well as guiding and supporting my team as I have described, I am also responsible for the long-term development of the Handelsbanken franchise here in our hometown.

Therefore, when it comes to staffing, it is my responsibility to ensure the branch has the level of resource, plus the mix of experience and skills we need to keep pace with our current and anticipated business growth.

For example, as the branch reached its fifth anniversary this year, not only did I need to recruit a second corporate manager, but I also felt confident that the knowledge and experience already in the branch would allow us to recruit a college-leaver—something we arranged ourselves liaising directly with the local sixth form college. This kind of initiative echoes the practice of UK banks almost a generation ago, where young people were recruited locally to learn 'retail banking' from grass roots level, rather than the more recent industry practice of learning in specific, narrow roles.

I believe this is a good example of how as a branch we are best able to track and adapt to the needs of our particular client base as it evolves over time. In this way, our customers form strong relationships with local bankers who both understand and can deal with the full range of services they require.

How we plan and review how we are doing. As far as more formal business planning goes in Handelsbanken, as branch manager I prepare an annual business plan with input from my whole team, and this is then shared with my regional manager. However, the discussion that follows is not one of "approval." Instead my regional manager offers a helpful sense-check that the aspirations we hold for our branch here are consistent with the aspirations of the region as a whole. There is no cajoling or demanding of higher targets, greater effort, more ambition, or anything like that. Indeed, just as I am careful not to seize ownership from, or demotivate, my own team members, so the regional manager is careful not to do this with me.

From day to day I am able to track our local business development through real-time access to financial information, made available in the bank's internal accounting systems. These systems have been designed specifically to support our decentralized approach, enabling me to track cost and income progression in fine detail. And since I can see this detail, I am able to quickly identify and address trends that have positive or negative potential for the branch.

Then, on a monthly basis, the bank makes available comparative reports on a range of key performance indicators, allowing me to gauge my branch's performance against that of my peer group, typically branches of a similar age. Again, this information is produced and made available to help me and all other branch managers adapt and improve our own performance over time, rather than being reported "up the chain" or used by head office to manage downwards. I can choose to follow up, act on, or ignore any part of it, since it is ultimately my responsibility to draw useful conclusions and judge appropriate ways forward for my branch.

Between branches we maintain a lively competition, with each of us striving to achieve the best cost-income ratio in our region. However, it is a healthy competition, with each of us always willing to share our own constructive experiences, or to seek specific insight from our peers, to the overall profit of the bank.

On an individual level, staff performance is formally assessed quarterly within the branch. This is part of an ongoing, annually renewed process that links an individual's own performance and development directly to the business plan and goals of the branch. The process starts with the branch's annual business plan, which is prepared by the team for the following year. This plan is effectively the sum of all the

Handelsbanken

specific initiatives detailed in each team member's own action plan, giving us confidence that we will succeed as a branch as long as everyone delivers the activities they have committed to.

And here I am talking about activities the team consider will achieve our agreed aspirations in terms of business growth, customer service, and administrative order, rather than being about attaining product volume or sales targets, as tends to be the focus elsewhere in the industry.

The quarterly reviews focus on the activities in each individual's action plan, their progress and effectiveness so far, whether any additional support is required, or whether we need to adapt our thinking in light of changing external conditions.

The lack of bonuses can mean that, from a solely economic point of view, a new recruit may earn less overall in their first year at Handelsbanken than they earned with their previous employer. However, I believe this is more than offset by the career prospects in Handelsbanken compared to other banks. Here, employees' salaries reflect their value to the organization as their skills, experience, and internal and external networks strengthen, rather than being matched against a central salary matrix. Then there is the everyday personal satisfaction of being a trusted decision-maker for the "best bank in town," as we see it.

Neither I nor any of my branch team believes what we are doing is rocket science; it's actually all fairly simple. But for now at least it appears only to be Handelsbanken that can deliver such a high level of local relationship banking service here in Colchester. In return we receive the trust, respect, and appreciation of our customers and the local professional community, proving it is not only satisfied customers our model creates, but satisfied bankers, too!

**

Again, my sincere thanks to Alan and Robin. This is an amazing story about the potential and the power of a management model working in line with and not against human nature, as Wallander put it. Although Wallander was clear that it is about much more than budgets, he was equally clear that the budget had to go. "The budget is in the best case totally unnecessary, and in the worst case actively harmful."

Key Takeaways

- Handelsbanken is unique in so many ways. No budgets, no targets, no individual bonus, and hardly any forecasting. Its early start in 1970 is also unique, in addition to its incredibly great performance ever since.
- Handelsbanken was not a tiny start-up able to maintain its agility, but a 100-year-old elephant that reinvented itself. None of today's agile transformations come close. No wonder the company is such an inspiration in the Beyond Budgeting community.
- The secret does not just lie in getting of rid of the budget, but in a unique understanding of the

---

importance of the management model and the conscious choice of building it in line with and not against human nature. This philosophy underpins the entire model, creating a strong coherence among all its elements.

- Alan Barnard gives us great insights into what the bank's model means in practice. Nothing beats an insider story from the ground.

Chapter 8

Implementation

H ere follows implementation advice drawn from Borealis, Equinor, and the many other organizations I have helped over the years. There is no rocket science, just simple insights about what worked and what didn't.

The Change Formula

Business literature is full of advanced change models. Every respectable consulting firm seem to have one. Most of them describe structured and orderly processes, typically sequential, and with a clear start and end.

In my experience, real change is different. It is often messy and iterative and has seldom a clear end. Afterwards, stories are often sanitized and presented as well planned and orderly successes.

There is, however, one model I do like. Not because it is called the *Change Formula* but because it has no steps. It only describes what must be in place for change to happen. The formula was developed by David Gleicher and later refined by Kathie Dannemiller. It simply says that

Dissatisfaction × Vision × First steps > Resistance

Any change requires a sufficient level of dissatisfaction with the current situation, a case for change as discussed next. But this is not enough; there must also be a compelling vision of something much better. Visions can sometimes feel like dreams, so there must also be some concrete first steps. The *product* of the three must be larger than the resistance. If any of the three are zero or close, resistance will always win.

We have addressed all three in this book. We started out with the problems and frustration about budgets and traditional management. We then looked at Beyond Budgeting as a visionary solution. Finally, we discussed budget purpose separation as a simple and effective way of getting started.

The Case for Change

Few, if any, are happy with the budgeting process. Even finance complains. As discussed, these problems are about much more than irritating itches. They are symptoms of a deeper and more systemic performance barrier problem. We must spend enough time helping the organization understand this. The more that people realize the underlying systemic nature of these problems, the stronger the case for change and the easier the implementation. Every time there is doubt about design choices, we can go back and test which solution will best solve the problems we identified.

Still, be careful with piling on too much criticism of what many managers feel comfortable with and maybe have no knowledge of something else. Some might even have built their career on traditional management. Help them instead understand that things have changed.

It is, however, not enough to be clear about the problems we are trying to solve. The case for change must also include what we aim for. In Borealis, we described this as decentralizing authority and decisions, improving financial management and performance evaluation, and simplifying and reducing time spent.

A Compelling Risk Picture

The biggest implementation barrier will always be fear: fear of cost increases, loss of control, and chaos and anarchy. Although 25 years of implementation history paints a very different picture, this nagging concern is certainly understandable.

I have wasted much energy arguing with skeptics claiming that costs will explode, control will be lost, and anarchy is next. My approach has changed. If it should go wrong, how big is the downside risk, really? It is close to zero! If it doesn't work, we can go back to the old way almost overnight. Nobody will have forgotten how to budget or all the other stuff! Even if we burned or deleted all instructions, nobody would have forgotten.

Compare this with the huge upside potential, as seen in so many great Beyond Budgeting cases. The risk picture is not scary; it is compelling.

Maybe we also should consider the risk of not doing this?

Up with the Umbrella

We often hear from people working in subsidiaries of large organizations that they would love to go Beyond Budgeting, but can't because the group is not convinced and keeps demanding budgets.

This doesn't have to be a showstopper. Even if there are such requirements from above, local management doesn't have to turn around and operate in exactly the same way inside their own organization. We have seen several examples of subsidiaries getting started on their own, both with and without permission from above. Local management puts up the umbrella and protects the organization from requirements from above, while practicing as much as possible of Beyond Budgeting internally. The protection job is mainly done by the subsidiary finance team.

This was what we did in Borealis. Our owners Statoil and Neste both had budgets. We just carved out the next calendar year from the five-quarter rolling forecast, renamed it *budget*, and sent it off. Fortunately, they were not too tight in their follow-up.

In some cases, local subsidiaries are allowed to start out as pilots. This can be a great way of learning and gaining knowledge and experience before a wider implementation.

The Viable Map

You might be familiar with the "Business Model Canvas," a popular concept and template used for documenting existing *business models* and developing new ones.

A similar concept for documenting and developing *management models* has so far not existed, but we have now developed one based on the Beyond Budgeting model. The Viable Map can be used to describe what a management model is, discuss what the current situation is, diagnose problems, and design a better way.

Why *viable*? It is about the ability to survive and thrive. Although we must perform well today, we must also make sure we adapt for the future.

It starts with an assessment of the organization's business environment. Where is it on a SUSO-VUCA scale (stable-understood-simple-obvious versus volatile-uncertain-complex-ambiguous)? The map describes alternatives for each of the six management processes, depending on the assessment. The higher the VUCA, the higher the need to move from fixed (traditional budgeting) to decoupled (purpose separation) via continuous (event/business driven rhythm) to relative (external perspectives).

The leadership assessment reflects the spirit of Douglas McGregor's Theory X and Theory Y. The development path here is more continuous, from X toward Y and more self-regulation, depending on how the organization view its employees. The focus on coherence is again key, internally between leadership messages and management practices, and externally between the organization adaptability and the VUCA level it operates under.

The model as illustrated in Figure 8.1 is not saying that being on the right is always best. It just says there must be coherence. If both the business environment and employees

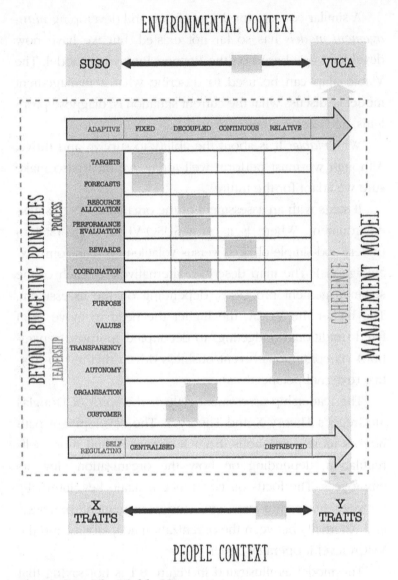

Figure 8.1 The Viable Map.
Source: Beyond Budgeting Institute.

are on the right, then this is where the management model must be. If the organization, however, operates in a SUSO environment and has done a lousy job in recruitment, then the left might be the place to be. There is still coherence. But there will then be other rather serious problems to deal with.

Check out the *Viable Map Workbook* to learn more. See bbrt.org for more information.

Start with Purpose Separation (but Never with Rolling Forecasts Only)

As discussed, budget purpose separation is a safe and tested way of getting started. Some start with rolling forecasts only because they regard this as the easiest of the three. This is, however, a classic mistake.

Some say they will replace budgets with rolling forecasts. Given the three budget purposes of target setting, forecasting, and resource allocation, this is meaningless. How will then target setting and resource allocation be handled? If it happens through a rolling forecast, the result is nothing but rolling budgets. If the budget is kept for these two purposes, a rolling forecast alone will solve very few of the many other budget problems discussed.

Separating target setting, forecasting, and resource allocation should therefore never be done sequentially. It must happen simultaneously. When rolling forecasts are introduced, the organization must at the same time also understand how target setting and resource allocation now will be done.

Design to 80% and Jump

The discomfort and uncertainty of leaving behind a well-known management model in favor of something new and unfamiliar leads many to believe that all new processes must, upfront, be designed down to the smallest detail to work.

This is a natural response to uncertainty: to try to design it away. When implementing Beyond Budgeting, we seldom know the exact right answer, and there is often more than one. It depends on the organization's business, history, and culture. Therefore, the solution can't be 100% predesigned and predefined. The only way to identify all challenges and issues is to get started. Find inspiration in the 12 principles and the intent of the model, but think and reflect about the right implications for your organization.

Agile advocates "minimum viable products," which provide early feedback about what works and what doesn't. Problems might very well occur in areas thought to be simple and safe.

It is important to be clear to the organization upfront about this approach being applied to avoid problems occurring being seen as mistakes and failures.

This does not mean that we can take shortcuts on understanding what Beyond Budgeting is about. The more that people understand, the better equipped they are for accepting challenges and helping in improving initial design solutions.

It is also important that the executive team think through what might go wrong to be prepared if it happens. This includes how to respond when trust is abused or when a good forecast with bad news is presented. Without such preparation, the responses will often be hectic and wrong.

Finance and Human Resources

Some finance people hesitate over our recommendation to team up with HR when implementing and operating Beyond Budgeting. The same goes for some HR people. There are, however, good reasons for the two functions to join forces. Working with cultural and behavioral changes is seldom a typical finance core competence. HR is also needed to ensure an integrated and seamless performance process all the way into HR territory of team and individual goal setting, evaluation, and rewards. It is important that these parts of the performance process also reflect and support the overall philosophy.

Unfortunately, there is sometimes tension between the two. They are not always the best of friends, and they sometimes talk more about each other than with each other. I know from personal experience because I have worked in both places. Theory Y messages from HR are easily killed by the opposite messages coming from finance, with budget control as a classic example.

This problematic relationship, however, can be turned into a great opportunity. Just like the two functions can block a transformation, they can also unlock it. Finance and HR are responsible for two of the most loathed corporate processes: budgeting and performance appraisals. Just as traditional budgeting is the antithesis of agile, the same can be said about many appraisal processes and connected reward systems. Making radical changes in one or both send an extremely powerful message to the organization that change is for real. Just as leaving them untouched carries the opposite message of no real change at all.

Join the BBRT

The Beyond Budgeting Roundtable (BBRT) is an international network of individuals and organizations being interested or being on the journey. The purpose of the network is to connect people and to help organizations learn from each other.

The Roundtable was established in 1998. We run an international conference twice a year, with an introduction session for people new to the concept and an implementers session for those having started, followed by a second day of a joint meeting with Beyond Budgeting case presentations and deep dives. We also run industry-specific networks for manufacturing, energy, NGOs, and others.

Hundreds of organizations have over the years been members. Beyond free conference participation, members also have access to more than 20 years of case studies, articles, and white papers.

We would love to have you onboard to learn, connect, and network. We are not a commercial machine, just a group of people passionate about a better way, and membership is as of today the main source of income to fund our activities.

Nobody Can Do It for You

Implementing Beyond Budgeting is not something that can be outsourced to management consultants. The organization itself must do the job.

This does not mean that help isn't needed. External support can provide inspiration, coaching, guiding and design ideas, and connections with other organizations on the journey, but those who will live with and operate the new model must always be in the driver seat. The higher the ambitions and the more transformation oriented it is, the more the executive level must take the lead. It can't be delegated.

As discussed, the Beyond Budgeting principles are just that—principles. It is not a one-size-fit-all recipe. The work on what these should mean in practice, and what to concretely do differently, must be led by those who know the business and the organization. The earlier this is understood and accepted, the higher the chance of a successful implementation.

The most valuable help is that which changes how people think. The most effective way of making this happen is called *normative change*, as recommended by, for instance, John Seddon and his Vanguard method. Here, people change how they think by observing in practice the dysfunctionality of the practices they have imposed. The Vanguard approach has been applied successfully in many service organizations, where executives, for instance, sit in and listen to customer calls and responses, having one "a-ha" moment after the other.

I strongly recommend executives, finance, and HR to engage with the organization to better understand how dysfunctional many of their current management processes really are.

Normative change differs from rational change, which is about using arguments to convince people, and coercive change, which is forced.

Only normative change delivers deep and sustainable change. Without it, the gravitation of the traditional way will make the organization drift back, often so slowly that few notice before it is too late.

I am fully aware that this book is mostly in the rational category because I haven't been able to be there with you, observing and discussing how things really work in your organization. I hope, however, that you have noticed how I repeatedly have stressed the need for also changing how we think.

Maybe I did change some hearts and minds? I really hope you didn't find me coercive!

Key Takeaways

- Although being skeptical to change formulas, the Change Formula makes sense to me. Any change requires a sufficient level of dissatisfaction and a compelling vision of something much better. The bridge between the two are concrete and tangible first steps.

- The implementation risk picture is compelling. So much upside, so little downside!
- Subsidiary or business unit heads often underestimate the autonomy and the power they have, even if levels above are skeptical or say no. Up with the umbrella!
- *The Viable Map* helps describe the current and desired management model, the gaps between the two, and how to close them. Check out the book!
- It is tempting to start with rolling forecasts only, but it is unfortunately a dead end. The three processes must be implemented in parallel, not sequentially.
- Design to 80% and jump. Change what doesn't work, continue with what does.
- Finance and HR should join forces and also the Beyond Budgeting Roundtable!
- No one can do this for you. Seek help for inspiration, guiding, and advice, but you can't delegate this.

Chapter 9
What's in It for the Bottom Line?

W e are, for good reasons, constantly asked for hard proof on how Beyond Budgeting improves the bottom line. Although absolute improvements, of course, can be measured, the challenge is how much to attribute to Beyond Budgeting as opposed to other tail- or headwind. Still, we do have some interesting data, which all paint quite a convincing picture.

Many start the journey thinking of the obvious cost savings they will get by eliminating bureaucracy, but they soon realize that the biggest benefit lies in the performance improvement that comes from being more adaptive, setting better targets, getting unbiased forecasts allowing for better decision-making, having a more efficient resource allocation and more engaged and motivated employees. Many of these effects are not easily identified on the bottom line.

Remember William Bruce Cameron's wise words: "Not everything that counts can be counted, and not everything that can be counted counts." We should always do what we believe is right, even if there are no immediate numbers to back it up.

Still, compelling evidence keeps emerging. Recently, Boston Consulting Group (BCG) did a study among Beyond Budgeting practitioners (Figure 9.1) on how the model affected their operations and performance. The most profound effect was financial, through an increase in sales, but many others reflected better quality and efficiency in affected management processes, which typically will translate into better financial results over time.

Almost 60% reported increased sales, and more than 50% reported lower cost in the process itself, better business decisions, and better agility in reallocating resources.

Beyond Budgeting in practice: Practitioners see significant benefits

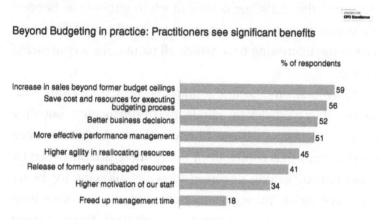

% of respondents

Increase in sales beyond former budget ceilings	59
Save cost and resources for executing budgeting process	56
Better business decisions	52
More effective performance management	51
Higher agility in reallocating resources	45
Release of formerly sandbagged resources	41
Higher motivation of our staff	34
Freed up management time	18

Figure 9.1   BCG study.
Note: Survey of finance executives having fully or partially implemented Beyond Budgeting (*n* = 174).
Source: BCG Center for CFO Excellence 2022 survey. All rights reserved.

The consulting firm Bain & Company ran a survey (Figure 9.2) among its finance clients, finding that leading firms in financial planning are much more likely to have adopted the Beyond Budgeting principles. There was a

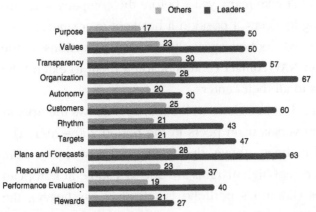

Leading firms in financial planning are much more likely to apply the Beyond Budgeting principles

Others   Leaders

	Others	Leaders
Purpose	17	50
Values	23	50
Transparency	30	57
Organization	28	67
Autonomy	20	30
Customers	25	60
Rhythm	21	43
Targets	21	47
Plans and Forecasts	28	63
Resource Allocation	23	37
Performance Evaluation	19	40
Rewards	21	27

Percentage of respondents who strongly agree that they adhere to these principles

Figure 9.2   Bain survey.
Note: (*n* = 236).
Source: Bain & Company February 2022 survey.

massive difference on most principles, both on leadership and management processes.

We have seen the remarkable effect Beyond Budgeting has had on Handelsbanken's performance, all the way back to the early 1970s: better returns than the average of its competitors, among the most cost-effective universal banks in Europe, outstanding customer satisfaction, and very high employee engagement. What more can one ask for?

Danish Coloplast develops products and services that make life easier for people with very personal and private medical conditions. The company employs 14,000 employees globally, with sales activities in 53 countries and production in Denmark, Hungary, France, China, and the United States.

Coloplast was for many years lagging behind its competitors, triggering a Beyond Budgeting implementation in 2009. It didn't take many years before the company was outperforming its peers, a position it has kept ever since.

Earlier, we looked at significant cost reductions at the Norwegian NAV contact centers, leading them to extend the two pilots to all their centers.

Equinor has also done well. Figure 9.3 shows the operating margin versus main peers in the period 2009–2021. The margin has been above these peers almost every year. Although recent high margins are due to a surge in European gas prices (Equinor's portfolio is relatively gas heavy), the strong relative performance over so many years give a pretty

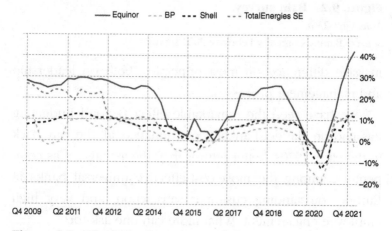

Figure 9.3 Equinor operating margin versus peers.
Source: Ekan Management.

This Is Beyond Budgeting

good indication. As you might remember, the company went Beyond Budgeting in 2005.

Again, I am not claiming that all of this can be tracked back to Beyond Budgeting, but it certainly hasn't hurt performance.

The savings from stopping doing "stupid stuff" are also considerable. The 2016 *Management Lab* article mentioned in Chapter 2 had a thorough analysis of the cost of US bureaucracy. The authors arrived at the staggering number of $3 trillion (!). "Since 1983, the number of managers, supervisors and support staff has nearly doubled, while employment in other occupations have grown by less than 40%."

These massive costs increases are, of course, about much more than budgets. Beyond Budgeting is not just challenging budgeting efforts but also the entire bureaucracy of traditional management.

The effects on recruitment have been discussed. People like to work for Beyond Budgeting companies. This has again positive effects on engagement for existing and new employees. As we will discuss in Chapter 10, going Beyond Budgeting changes work in a very positive way, making it more meaningful and fulfilling.

The fact that so few go back once they have started also indicates that organizations sense and realize Beyond Budgeting benefits even if they sometimes may be hard to single out, measure, and prove.

Key Takeaways

- Improvement effects are often difficult to measure, which doesn't mean they don't exist.
- BCG and Bain & Company surveys report significant benefits.
- A *Management Lab* study puts the cost of excessive US bureaucracy at $3 trillion.
- Although a company like Handelsbanken has a long history of outperforming peers, companies starting later, such as Equinor, Coloplast, and many others, are also building impressive track records.
- Still, "Not everything that counts can be counted, and not everything that can be counted counts."

Chapter 10

What's in It for Me?

G oing Beyond Budgeting changes work and has consequences for many roles. If you are an executive, a
manager, or if you work in finance or HR, should you be
worried? No, you need not be. Your job will change, but to
the better. It will become much more meaningful and
fulfilling.

It will be less about managing and more about enabling.
It will be about dismantling organizational traffic lights,
replacing them with roundabouts where self-regulation, trust,
autonomy, transparency, and collaboration is key. The result
will be a much better flow, more engaged employees, and
much better performance. There is not much to be worried about!

Executive roles are becoming more strategic, but also
more people-oriented. There will be more coaching and
guidance, and fewer instructions. There will be more credibil-
ity in corporate leadership messages when employees experience a new coherence between what is said and what is
done. The organization will become more adaptive and more
human, and will perform better, in the right way.

There will also be less room for "managerial laziness" through dangling carrots and mechanical performance evaluations. This may even apply for those on the receiving end of it. Maybe some deep down appreciate being told exactly what to do, what to deliver, and what to spend.

The laziness here lies in being uncomfortable about making decisions under uncertainty, appreciating that these are being elevated upstairs. I can understand that. But this doesn't make uncertainty disappear. It has just been moved up where it might be even more difficult to know what the right decisions are and what kind of performance has been delivered. However, it makes life below more comfortable and predictable, even if there still might be complaints about all the decisions and verdicts being made upstairs.

The middle manager role also will change in other ways. There will be fewer of them, but instead of being squeezed between corporate demands and employee resistance, conflicts and frustration will be replaced with more autonomy and more common agendas.

Finance will experience fewer annual stunts and more forward-looking and less backwards-looking work. The role also becomes less finance and more business oriented. There will be less functional silos and more collaboration. The image of finance in the organization will improve. Few will miss the old days. I can't recall a single finance person in Equinor looking back longingly.

HR will experience a similar image boost. Leadership training will become more credible and relevant due to a new coherence between what is said and what is done.

The quality of recruitment candidates will improve. People like to work for Beyond Budgeting organizations.

It won't be easier, though. It takes more leadership, and not just from those in formal leadership roles. It requires accepting uncertainty and ambiguity in ways seldom needed in more traditional regimes.

What we have discussed in this book will happen, in some form or shape. Maybe you wonder why it is taking so long? Don't forget that budgeting was invented 100 years ago but didn't become mainstream before after the Second World War. And it took quite some time before agile started to creep into corporate agendas.

As we have learned, it is already happening. "The future is already here, it's just not very evenly distributed," as William Gibson put it.

It won't stop here. Guaranteed. I don't care if it will be called Beyond Budgeting, or Business Agility, or whatever. That is not important.

When in 15–20 years' time we look back at today's main-stream management thinking, we will all smile, maybe have a laugh, just like we today smile about the time before the internet. It isn't that long ago. I hope the public sector will be there with us, having a good laugh about something that used to be called new public management.

Organizations have a choice. They can be early movers, embracing management innovation because they understand it brings competitive advantage. Or they can end up as lag-gards, dragged in as one of the last. The longer one waits, the more competitors will be ahead.

Maybe you also have a choice. Maybe you will be among those remembered for making this happen in your organization. Or for the opposite if you resisted. Or forgotten if you didn't take a stand.

Whatever you decide, I wish you all the best. Thank you for finding the time to read this book.

Epilogue

You will often have heard me talking about "we." So, who are we?

Beyond Budgeting has a tripartite structure.

The Beyond Budgeting Institute (BBI) is together with the Core Team (see following) responsible for maintaining and developing the Beyond Budgeting model. BBI publishes books, whitepapers, and articles. Rikard Olsson from Swedish EKAN is the current managing director.

The Beyond Budgeting Roundtable (BBRT) is a knowledge-sharing membership network. Many members are already on the journey, many join to learn. BBI and BBRT organize global, regional, and industry-specific conferences and meetings. I am the chairman of BBRT.

Beyond Budgeting Advisory (BBA) delivers advisory services, either directly from Core Team members or by working with national Beyond Budgeting partners or others.

The Core Team is made up of people representing the founders, Beyond Budgeting partners, and thought leaders. The group is also referred to as the official Beyond Budgeting leaders. The current members are Franz Röösli, Steve Morlidge, Anders Olesen, Dag Larsson, and me.

I am forever grateful for knowing and for working with these guys, and for so long, some for almost 30 years. We have learned from each other; we have challenged each other, and there has never been a bad word between us. We all believe that one day these ideas will become the way, not just the new way. We have never been closer.

Whatever happens next, nobody can take away what we have achieved so far. We have already made a difference, a positive difference.

"If you want to travel fast, travel alone. If you want to travel far, travel together."

Index

Page numbers followed by *f* refer to figures.

culture of, 114–117
digital strategy of, 106
Hesselberg, Jorgen, 94
High Output Management
(Grove), 96
Hilti, 71
Hock, Dee, 56–57, 73
Hope, Jeremy, 2, 7, 28
Humanocracy (Hamel and
Zanini), 88
Human resources (HR):
in design of performance
process, 32, 33
and finance function, 34, 131
in implementation, 131–132
role change for, 144–145
use of term, 17
The Human Side of Enterprise
(McGregor), 31
Hurtigruten, 87

I
If, 71
Illusion of control, 12–13, 13*f*
Implementation, 123–135
and case for
change, 124–125
external support for,
133–134
finance and human
resources in, 131–132
as improvements vs. as
transformations, 78–79
purpose separation in, 129
*Implementing Beyond
Budgeting* (Bogsnes), 4
Improvers, 78–79
Innovation paradox, 11

Intel, 96
Internal benchmarking,
43, 44
Intrinsic motivation, 70–71

K
Key performance indicators
(KPIs), 66–67
guiding on, 47–48
at Handelsbanken, 108, 119
and objectives and key
results, 97
Kohn, Alfie, 71
Kontor Syd, 72
KPIs, *see* Key performance
indicators

L
Larsen, Diana, 94, 96
Larsson, Dag, 147
Leadership:
in implementation, 133
in the public sector, 80
role changes in, 145
Leadership principles, 33*f*
coherence of management
processes and, 33–34, 33*f*
origins of, 34–39
Theory Y, 31–32
on Viable Map, 127, 128*f*
Lean, 5, 93
Learning, 42–43

M
McGregor, Douglas, 31, 127
McKinsey, James O., 22–23
Maersk Group, 71
Maersk Tankers, 71